Contents

FRESHMAN

13

SOPHOMORE

41

JUNIOR

SENIOR

101

TERMINOLOGY

145

INDEX

199

UNDERSTANDING
COMPUTERS

... in a weekend

DOT Publishing

Post Office Box 1148
Friday Harbor, WA 98250-1148

Printed and published in the
United States of America.

DOT Publishing

P.O. Box 1148
Friday Harbor, WA 98250-1148

First Printing ....July 1992
Revised 2nd Edition.................................. April 1993
Revised 3rd Edition............................ February 1995

📖

ISBN 0-9629304-3-1

Catalog Card Number: 95-92094

Cataloging in Publication Data

Traynor, David O.
    Understanding Computers : -- in a weekend /
    David Traynor. --
  3rd ed.
    208p. 20.5 cm.
    Includes index.
    Pre-assigned LCCN: 95-92094.
    1. Computers.   I. Title

If you think the *insiders* can predict the future, consider these quotes:

[1943] "I think there is a world market for about five computers".
Thomas Watson, CEO of IBM

[1977] "There is no reason for any individual to have a computer in his or her own home".
Kenneth Olsen, CEO of Digital Equipment Corporation (DEC)

Disclaimer
While every effort has been made to ensure the contents of this book are accurate, neither the publisher, author, or his agents will accept liability for any inaccuracy contained herein.

The following terms are used extensively in this book to describe various aspects of computers. They are Trade Marks™ of their respective companies: *i386, i486, Pentium* processor- int_el® Corp.; *System 7* - Apple; *040* - Motorola; *MS-DOS, Excel, Word* - Microsoft® Corp.; *1-2-3* - Lotus® Development Co.; *PageMaker* - Aldus Corp.

Copyright © 1995
by David O. Traynor

Man is still the most extraordinary computer of all.

John F. Kennedy
May 21, 1963

Produced with
Word for Windows
and *Ami Pro.*

The text and most of the graphics for this book were printed "camera ready" with a Hewlett Packard LaserJet 4M printer, using Adobe PostScript fonts. The result is 600 dpi (dots per inch) quality compared to 1280 or 2450 for professional offset. This book is an illustration of the capabilities of a **desktop publishing** system. **Speech Recognition** technology was used to revise this third edition.

Front cover illustration is by Vaughn Aldredge and Suzy Wilson.
Internal illustrations are by Stacey George, Joel West, and application clipart.

A grateful thank you to my Father for his encouragement in this career, and to my Mother and sister Carole for their encouragement in the publication of this book.

A special note of thanks to Dorothy Rasmussen for her very careful and thorough editing of the original manuscript.

A special thank you to Timothy Thompson for his technical advice, and thank you to those who read part or all of the manuscript before its publication and offered helpful suggestions and corrections.

We wish to acknowledge and thank Dr. Burton Smith, Chief Scientist at Tera Computer, for his time and answers to specific technical questions.

About this book ...

✔   The *tutorial* section is divided into four chapters: **Freshman, Sophomore, Junior,** and **Senior.** These chapters explain the *ins and outs* of *Personal Computers.*

✔   The **Terminology** section, beginning on page 145, is an alphabetical listing explaining all the terms you are likely to come across in the world of *Personal Computers.*

✔   The **Index,** beginning on page 199, is a cross-reference listing of *all* the subjects and terms in the book by page number. It's the *fastest* way to find an answer.

> **Bold face words** and other selected terms
>
> are cross-referenced in the **INDEX**.

Computers are fun ... ☺

they're also confusing, fascinating and essential ... ☺

➡️   *Computers are fun, right?   At times, they're also confusing, fascinating and essential. When you use the phone, receive money with your ATM (Automatic Teller **Machine**) card, pay with a credit card, or cook with a microwave, a computer is involved.   Many cameras, washing and sewing machines, memory typewriters, automobiles, and digital watches, all utilize a miniature "computer on a chip" ... not all computers are PCs sitting on a desk.   Pocket-sized electronic organizers, such as those made by Casio and Sharp, also operate with a "computer on a chip".*

☯ Making the Impossible, *Possible* ...

From history we realize that we have always employed tools and machines to assist us in our work. A cart drawn by a horse can haul a lot of hay, and a lever under a two-ton rock can be used to do what would be impossible for ten men ... move it. A cart without wheels is just a box, so it's the *wheels*, that turn it into a *useful machine*.

The horse has been replaced by an engine, and the cart is now called a truck. We have cranes and hydraulic lifts to do what levers used to do, but remember they built the mighty Pyramids of Egypt four thousand years ago with levers, carts, and a lot of muscle.

Notches in stone and marks on papyrus were used to calculate amounts owed and quantities of wheat stored. The Chinese Abacus greatly improved this, and our modern slide rule offered extraordinary accuracy, but calculating with numbers was cumbersome until a calculating machine, complete with cogs and spokes, was invented. Mechanical calculators, the first *"number crunchers"*, were replaced by electronic computers, only recently

Typesetting in the 15th century gave us printed books, and it took almost 400 years for that to be miniaturized down to a personal typesetter, better known as a typewriter. Today we can draft a letter on screen, spell check it, and print unlimited numbers with printing press quality. And now, with **Speech Recognition** technology, we can even *talk* to our computer!

It is these two capabilities that lie at the heart of the modern-day computer: working with numbers and words.

➤ What is a Computer?

Let's start with a simple question ... just what is a computer? Someone or *something* that computes, *is a **computer***! Sounds silly, doesn't it? Prior to World War II the word applied to a person, usually one of hundreds in a large room, laboriously calculating numbers.

In its broadest definition an electronic computer is a machine; yes, that's right, it's a *machine*. It's a machine because it is an *inanimate* object which *assists humans* in their work. What makes it unique, compared with all other machines, is that the use or application is determined by you. The name ***IBM*** includes a clear reference to the word (International Business *Machines), though they never dreamed it would be anything but a business machine.*

Normally, when we use the word ***computer***, we are referring to an electronic machine, which follows a preset list of instructions; but does it have to be electronic? The answer is no. The ancient *abacus* is an early computer which is still used in various parts of the world today to make mathematical calculations, and in the hands of a proficient operator, it can give the result faster than a hand-held electronic calculator. The modern *slide rule* is also an example of a computer.

The most prevalent type of computers are simple electro-mechanical *(analog)* computers such as your car's speedometer and the electric utility meter that is used by the power company to measure your usage. The retail cash register is an example of a mechanical (*digital*) computer. It totals your purchases, figures the sales tax if applicable, and totals the day's cash receipts, often by category. We'll discuss the difference between *analog* and *digital* a little further on.

A pulley is a machine that offers mechanical advantage; an electronic computer offers an advantage of *SPEED*. In other words, it is doing something we could otherwise do by the use of our own brain following a set of memorized rules. While early computers were used to only solve complex mathematical problems, today's PCs use their processing power for an infinite variety of useful functions.

The technical definition of a modern digital computer is a machine that stores a set of instructions (a program) for processing data and then executes those instructions upon request.

Though computers are machines they are unique in the world of machines in one very extraordinary way: they are not pre-designed to perform a specific function ... in fact, until the software is loaded, a computer can't do a thing!

Let's take an automobile for example, as it is a machine with which we are all very familiar. A car is used to travel much faster than we could walk, or ride for that matter. In addition, the car can carry heavy loads without sacrificing speed. But suppose a river lies in our path ... we all know a car doesn't float ... suddenly our car is useless! We need another machine, such as a ferry, to *float* the car across the river. Each machine is *designed* to perform a single or narrow range of functions. A ferry would look pretty silly trying to *motor* down the highway.

As useful as a cash register is, it will always be just that. The factor that separates modern electronic computers is their ability to utilize an infinite number of different sets of instructions (software), which gives the computer an infinite number of applications.

A computer is not built with a dedicated end use. The same computer utilizing different programs (software) can make an airline reservation, send an elevator to the 100th floor without stopping because its sensors detect the car is full, relay satellite imagery to Earth, control the washing machine cycle, *crunch* numbers, play music, or display images such as pictures, on a computer screen.

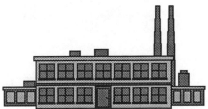

When we think of machines we often think of a factory because it usually contains so many powerful machines ... but the most powerful machine of all, is a *Computer*.

➤ What's a PC? ⌨

It's short for *Personal Computer*. The expression was coined in 1981 by IBM to differentiate their new *microcomputer* from the company's existing line of computers designed for *many* users accessing the computer simultaneously. People commonly refer to *IBM* compatibles as *PCs*, and *Apple/Macintosh* computers as *Macs*. All computers that are designed to be used by a *single* user are *personal* computers.

➤ What's a Pentium?

It's the name of a **microprocessor** model, or *computer on a chip*. The *micro*, or "tiny" *processor*, normally called the CPU (Central Processing Unit), is the PCs *brain* or *engine*. The

Pentium was released in 1993, and is 2½ times faster than its predecessor, the *486*! It is the called a *Pentium* if it's made by int℮l, and *586* if it's made by another computer chip manufacturer. int℮l gave its *486* successor a name, *"Pentium™ Processor"*, to distinguish it from its competitors, who use the same model numbers (386, 486). *Pentium's* successor, the **P6** (*686CPU*), has already been announced by int℮l for late '95. The illustration depicts the size of a typical CPU.

What's a 486? It's a little bit like describing a car by its engine size. *"486"* expressed as *"4-86"*, is derived from the *i80486* (*int℮l 80-4-86*). The *IBM PC* and its rival clones <u>were</u> based on a line of CPUs, or *engines*, manufactured by int℮l. *IBM*, *AMD*, *Cyrix* and *NexGen* also manufacture microprocessors that will run *DOS/Windows* software, in some cases, out perform their int℮l counterpart. Most *PC*s sold today are powered by the *i486 chip*, but this will shift to the *586/Pentium*, at least in the US, as the price of the *Pentium* is lowered.

Apple computers use the *Motorola 6800*, and the ***Macintosh*** series use the *Motorola 68000* family of microprocessors. The *PowerPC* uses a new *Motorola* CPU chip: the 601, 603 and 620.

<u>*History:*</u>   The original *IBM PC* started with the int℮l 8088/8086 *chip* in 1981. The *IBM AT* and *Compaq 286* are based on the int℮l *80286*, better known as the *286*, which became the second generation of *IBM PCs* in 1984. *Compaq*

introduced the first really powerful PC, based on the *386* CPU in 1986, beating *IBM* to the market by eight months.

IBM debuted its *386* in 1987, to regain its leadership lost to *Compaq*, and market share to the less expensive clones.   The PS/2 line introduced the 3½" **diskette** drive, **VGA** graphics monitor, and the proprietary **MCA bus** design. The <u>fourth generation</u> int_el *80486 ("486")* arrived in '89 with a less fanfare, but offered significant performance improvements.

➤ What's the difference between Hardware 🖥️⌨️ and Software? 💾📇

Hardware refers to the computer and its related equipment: generally, things you can see and touch.   Hardware includes the computer, screen, keyboard, and any related devices such as the printer, modem, and scanner. A fax machine would not be considered computer hardware, unless it is an *internal fax board*.

Software, while it comes on a *diskette*, is invisible to the user, until it's installed. *Software* programs, or instructions, are the *language* of computers, that allow it to perform all the wonderful functions. We use English, spoken or written, to communicate. Examples of software are the computer's *Operating System,* aka

DOS (more about that later), and programs such as *1-2-3, Excel, Word,* and *WordPerfect.*

> *Without software, a computer is just an organized mass of silicon chips and electronic devices, which cannot perform any useful task.*

If the concept of software is still fuzzy, think of it this way: Think of the process you go through when you give someone directions to drive to your home. Imagine those directions, or *instructions*, have to be very detailed because the person is not familiar with your area and there are lots of tricky forks in the road. That's essentially what a program is: a *detailed list of instructions* telling the computer what to do.

It's a *software program* that guides the *Shuttle* into space and back again, interprets the pilot's commands in *fly-by-wire* aircraft (especially fighters), routes phone calls across town, the nation and around the world, and prints a detailed grocery receipt, giving a description and cost of each item. While the same computer hardware could be employed in each case, different programs or software would be needed: it is the software instructions that control all the computer's varied functions.

➤ The parts of a Computer

This is the *Hardware* side of computers. The actual micro-processor or **CPU** (Central

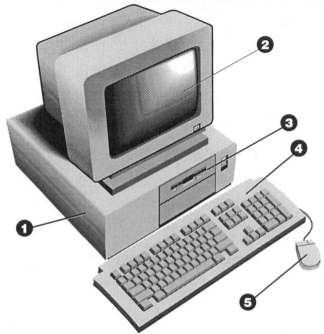

Processing Unit), which is after all a *computer on a chip*, hardly constitutes what we generally mean when we refer to a computer. We are referring to a complete system, and it takes a few other parts to make the computer really useful.

The principal devices, or parts of a computer system, are listed in bold type followed by a simple explanation of their function.

☑ **External Illustration:**

❶ **Computer box** ....This houses most of the parts of a computer and it is the location where the computer actually does its *work*. The largest component inside is the mainboard, better known as the **motherboard**, to which all the components are connected. The **CPU** and the memory chips are generally located on the motherboard. The computer box also houses the internal **disk** drives.

❷ **Monitor**...............Similar to a small household TV, it is the *Output* device which displays what we enter, and in turn it displays the computer's response.

❸ **Disk Drive** .... An *Input/Output* (I/O) device which *reads* **software** and user files into memory from a magnetically encoded **disk**. As an output device it *writes* to the disk thereby making a permanent record of the user's work. Usually the **diskette** drive and the **Hard Disk** are installed next to each other. It's like a small CD player that can *record* and *playback*.

❹ **Keyboard**............This is the computer's primary *Input* device enabling us to *communicate* with the computer. Someday this will be obsolete, but only when we can give *all* our commands by *talking* to the computer.

❺ **Mouse**................ ⊕ The fun little hand-held, screen, *point-and-click* device which bypasses some of the keyboard input operations ↳⊚.

Printer....................The computer's secondary *Output* device which gives us a permanent copy, often called a *hard* copy. This is discussed in **Which Printer is right for me?**, in the **Senior** chapter.

☑ Internal Illustration:

❶ Motherboard......This is a large circuit board upon which all the computer's internal parts are interconnected, including the **CPU**, **RAM** memory chips, power supply, system clock, and the expansion **slots**. The internal **disk drives** are connected by a special cable. The CPU (illustrated), RAM, Coprocessor and clock chips all plug into the motherboard.

❷ Expansion Board.........Also known as *expansion card*, which allows additional capabilities to be added anytime to a computer. *Expansion boards* offer features such as sharper video graphics, an additional hard drive, or a fax modem. Every computer normally has one *board* installed for the video display.

❸ Expansion Slot .... This is where *Expansion Boards* are plugged in, allowing the computer to access the *board's* features. The illustration depicts three *full-size* and one *half-size* expansion slots. The first full-size slot shows an *expansion board* inserted.

❹ Port ....Cables from external or **peripheral** devices, such as a printer and mouse, are connected to the computer via a (serial or parallel) *port*. The *ports* are accessed from the rear of the computer.

❺ Power Supply .....This converts the incoming AC electricity (from the wall plug) into low voltage DC current (3.3 to 5 volts) which is what

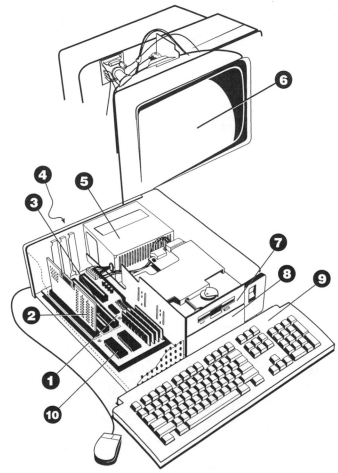

the computer requires. The *power supply* is rated according to its output, typically 90 to 300 watts. Its wattage rating must be adequate to support existing components and any **expansion boards** that are added.

❻ Monitor...............Also known as a RGB (red/green/blue) monitor or a CRT (Cathode Ray

Tube). It is similar to a color TV screen. Details are discussed in the **Senior** chapter.

❼ **Diskette Drive** .. This is the internal *diskette drive*. A 3.5" drive is illustrated, however it could also be a 5.25" disk drive. An option (not shown) is an internal tape backup system.

❽ **Hard Drive** .... An internal *Hard Disk Drive*. Typically these range from 40 **megabytes** of storage capacity to 300 **MB**. It is also called *Fixed Disk* as it *fixed* inside.

❾ **Keyboard** .... An enhanced 101-key *keyboard* is illustrated. It features 12 function keys across the top, a separate number pad and separate cursor-control arrow keys.

❿ **RAM memory** .... Plug-in memory *chips* which are normally measured in megabytes (MB). This is the computer's temporary memory area where all the active programs and data are held ready for the CPU to access. This is explained in detail in the **Junior** chapter.

➤ What's a Keyboard for? ⌨

It's to communicate with the computer. A computerese definition is, "it's the primary *Input* device".

Practical typewriters and their familiar keyboards have been around since the late 1800s

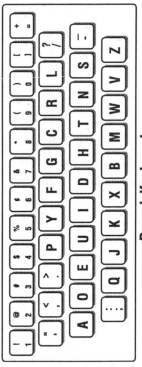

Dvorak Keyboard

but it wasn't until recently that typewriter keyboards were attached to computers. Why?

Even in the early 1970s, a million dollar *IBM 370* mainframe used *punched cards*, 3" x 7" cards with rectangular holes, to enter instructions. The punch card technology was introduced by an Englishman named Charles Babbage (1792-1871), who adapted the system from the textile industry. A hole through which light or a mechanical pin passed represented a *one*, and an unpunched spot represented a *zero*. A typewriter-like keyboard was used to create the punch cards but the keyboard was not connected directly to the computer. Converting programming instructions into punch cards was slow, and not at all user friendly.

The computer keyboard is an electronic adaptation of the typewriter. Early typewriters used a sensible keyboard which placed the most commonly used letters together. As typewriters improved and speed increased, the mechanical arms began jamming, as they could not fall back into place quickly enough. The engineers solved this problem by so arranging the keyboard as to *slow down* the typist! *Voilà* what we call the *QWERTY* keyboard (from the first five letters of the top row).

August Dvorak tried to remedy this with the *Dvorak* keyboard which allowed about 75% of the letters to be typed using only the middle row of keys, but the *Depression* and *QWERTY* habit killed it. Unfortunately, because the *QWERTY* keyboard was so well entrenched, it is with us to this day and is the slowest and most error prone part of entering data into the computer. **Speech recognition** systems are finally a practical reality and offer the first true "human interface".

KeyTronic Corporation makes a variety of after-market keyboards, and some keyboard manufacturers offer (software) **driver**s to convert your existing keyboard to Dvorak, or foreign language layouts.

 **Around the KEYBOARD**

The **Function keys, F1** through **F12**, offer a faster way of accessing commonly used commands such as HELP, GOTO, SAVE, and SPELL. **F1** is usually the HELP command, and **F5** is typically the GOTO command. The use of the "F keys" is assigned by each program, though some allow you to reassign the "F keys".

"Shift+" means *press and hold* the ⇧Shift key, while pressing another key. NUM LOCK does not refer to the state you are often in when trying to figure out what the computer is doing: it's to toggle between the number pad and the direction keys!

~ .....*Tilde* ....Top left corner

#......*Pound* or *number symbol* ..Above "3"

^......*Carrot*................................Above "6"

& .....*Ampersand (="and")* ....Above "7"

*......*Asterisk*..............................Above "8"

( )...*Parenthesis*, left and right.Above "9 and 0"

[ ]...*Bracket*, left and right ....Right of "P"

{ }..*Brace*, left and right ....Right of "P"

- .....*Hyphen*................................. Right of "Zero"

_......*Underscore* ....Top right, above the Hyphen

< >...*Less than, greater than* .....Lower right

\ / ....*Back slash* and *forward slash* .Lower right

0......*Zero* ....Top right

Oo ..*Oh*, upper and lower case.

➤ **What's a Mouse?** 🖱 📷

   Most people like to point with their finger, but a computer doesn't have "eyes" to see where you are pointing to on the screen, so a special gadget is needed. By moving a small hand-held device, dubbed a "mouse", around on a desk you can make corresponding movements to a screen "cursor", a small moveable arrowhead ↘↗, thus telling the computer where you want to start typing text, begin a drawing, or select a command from a list (called a "menu"). It bypasses the normal keyboard entry method of typing, for many operations. This is used to *point* to a menu command or little icons, representing such things as the *print command* and to start **application** programs.   Freehand movements of your mouse on the desktop, result in corresponding movements by the arrowhead on screen.   All *Windows*, *Apple/Mac* and some DOS applications support a mouse.

There are few types: a regular *mouse*, ⇔ 🖱 ⇕

which you move around, a *Trackball* type 🖲, where the *mouse* remains stationary and your finger rolls a ball built into the top of the mouse to move the arrowhead, stationary mouse pads which now come built-into laptops, and cordless mice which come close to having the feel of pointing with your finger.   The difference is primarily personal preference, however if clear desk space is limited the *mouse pad or cordless* is preferable. Most models have two buttons, a few have three, however the use of the buttons is determined by the particular software application. The expression *"to click on [something]"* is used in relation to these buttons. *Clicking* on an icon or menu item that the arrowhead is on is usually the equivalent of pressing the Enter key.

A *mouse* is considered essential in drawing programs and greatly facilitates the copying and moving of text in a **word processing** program.

Not all Mice are the same ... *Cordless* mice such as *RemotePoint* by *InterLink* offer the greatest flexibility, while *Pen* mice and *Trackballs* are clumsy for *click-and-drag* operations. The *RemotePoint* works from any comfortable position, much like pointing a TV remote. *Microsoft* makes the most popular *mouse* and *Logitech* offers some neat ergonomic designs. *KeyTronic*'s *Lifetime* mouse can use *any* surface, even glass, and doesn't pick up dirt particles from the surface, causing erratic screen pointer movements. Buying a new *laptop*? Consider IBM's tiny red "joystick" mouse located in the center of the keyboard, or the new built-in "mouse pad" which moves the screen pointer by corresponding movements of your fingertip around the pad (*GlidePoint* makes an external pad).

➤ What is a "byte" or kilobyte?

Fortunately it has no reference to being *bitten*. A computer works with just two possibilities in all the functions it performs: a simple "*yes/no*" world, expressed as numbers:

"*1 or 0*". Before a computer can act on an instruction, it must understand that instruction: a computer understands *bytes*, not words or decimal numbers. *Bytes* are the language of computers just as *words* are the language of humans. When you press the letter "A", the computer converts that keyboard signal to an 8-digit number: "01000001". This 8-digit binary number is called a "byte". It is called a "binary number" to differentiate it from our normal "decimal numbers" (0,4,5,6...9). One thousand of these 8-digit numbers is a "*kilo*byte". *Kilo* is the Greek word for thousand, and *kilobyte* therefore, is simply a shorter way of saying *"one thousand bytes"*. A *kilobyte* is actually 2^{10} or 1,024 bytes, as it is a binary, not decimal number.

Each of the eight "0s and 1s" in a *byte* is called a "*bit*". The word "*bit*" is derived from two words: "BInary digiT". Just as we use various combinations of letters, from *a* to *z*, to make up words, so a computer uses combinations of 0s, and 1s, to make its language. This is a visualization of a computer's binary language:

Binary Code for "a":	0	1	1	0	0	0	0	1
Electronic Circuits:	OFF	ON	ON	OFF	OFF	OFF	OFF	ON

Binary Code for "Z":	0	1	0	1	1	0	1	0
Electronic Circuits:	OFF	ON	OFF	ON	ON	OFF	ON	OFF

Although a single-digit *bit* is the smallest piece of data a computer uses, an eight-digit *byte* is the smallest executable piece of information a computer can understand, as it is equivalent to a single letter or number (e, Z, 5). Every upper and lower case letter of the alphabet, punctuation marks, numbers, etc., is assigned an eight-digit binary number (defined by **ASCII**). A *byte* is also used to measure the computer's capacity, both its *working* memory (RAM), and its disk memory. When the *PC* has a RAM capacity of 2 megabytes, it is commonly known as *"a 2-meg computer"*. A **megabyte**, is a million bytes.

➤ History of Computers

➠ The following is not essential reading but may be of assistance in your understanding of the gradual development of computers.

The earliest computers were entirely mechanical as electricity had not been discovered. They resembled hundreds of old-fashioned clock wheels with cogs and drums, all mounted on numerous axles, and turned by a handle.

In Germany, during the 1930s, Konrad Zuse produced the first practical electric computer (Z1-Z4), and by 1939

was considered the world's leader in the field of computers. As Hitler saw no immediate benefits from computers, he dropped government funding in 1942, and thereafter the US took center stage.

As in Europe the primary impetus for development of computers in the USA came from the military. Days, weeks and even months were needed to calculate artillery firing tables ... something which was vital, but it competed with the existing shortages in the labor market.

The first successful general-purpose computer, known as the *Mark I*, was developed by a Harvard mathematician named Howard Aiken under IBM's patronage in <u>1943</u>. It was electromechanical and therefore inherently slow, taking almost three seconds to multiply two numbers. Its existence was not revealed until 1944 when it was leased to the US Navy. It did calculations in a single day that had previously taken six months. After the war it was returned to Harvard, where it continued in operation for sixteen years.

A quantum leap in speed was achieved in <u>1945</u> with the introduction of the US Army funded *ENIAC* Computer (Electronic Numerical Integrator and Calculator), which used vacuum tubes. Zuse (Germany) had first proposed using vacuum tubes but was prevented from developing a working model when government funding was cut off. It took just 3/1,000 of a second to do the same function as the *Mark I*, a 1,000% improvement!

The British also made extensive use of computers for code breaking during *World War II*, under a secret program named *Colossus*. In 1949 Maurice Wilkes (UK) made an important breakthrough by storing the computer's instructions (software) internally. In the same year Zuse began manufacturing a successor to the Z4 in Germany.

Computers developed in the 1940s, '50s and '60s are classed as <u>First Generation Computers</u> as they used hundreds of vacuum tubes just like early family radios. The vacuum tubes were connected by thousands of wires to relay switches that made for a very complicated machine. Additionally it needed a very large room and a team of technicians to keep it going as the vacuum tubes burned out.

The world's first commercial computer was LEO (Lyon's Electronic Office) which entered service in the UK a few months before UNIVAC. It was used to calculate the weekly payroll for Lyons, which operated a chain of English tearooms.

The first mass-produced computer, the UNIVAC I (UNIVersal Automatic Computer), was introduced in <u>1951</u>. By 1956, IBM, driven by Tom Watson, Sr.'s superior marketing strategy, was the industry leader. Bank of America once estimated that if it had not introduced computers, it would have employed every clerk in California to cope with their workload. The commercial jet-age also began in this decade, and in 1959 Boeing delivered the first Presidential jetliner.

Transistors or semiconductors (see Terminology section), which were invented in the U.S. in 1948, began to replace vacuum tubes in the 1960s, and this heralded the Second Generation Computer. Transistors greatly reduced the size of the computer, increased its speed and reliability, and made it less costly to mass-produce.

However, the real breakthough came with the introduction of Integrated Circuits, or **IC**s. Although they were invented in 1958, they were not utilized immediately because of their high cost. However, when the US Government needed computers for space craft, small size and weight were more important than cost. The rest is history. Computers utilizing **IC**'s became known as the Third Generation of Computers, and this is what we mean when we refer to [modern] computers.

The IBM PC wasn't the first personal computer, but it did start the revolution that has so changed our society through the widespread use of personal computers. The title of *first* belongs to the *MITS Altair*, which was featured on the cover of *Popular Electronics* in 1975. This was followed soon after by the *Apple I* and *Apple II*, the *Commodore PET*, the *TRS-80* and the *Osborne* among others.

Each personal computer in those days had its own Operating System, its own application programs, and to top it off, its own user interface! This meant users had a confusing array of choices with no ability to transfer information from one system to another.

Along came *Big Blue* (IBM) with the muscle to set standards for the personal computer, such as the all-important Operating System. IBM selected *Microsoft's* Disk Operating System, better known as *DOS*, and offered "open" hardware and software standards, enabling software developers to write a wide variety of **applications**, such as *WordStar*, *SuperCalc*, and *1-2-3*.

When Alfred P. Sloan was building GM into the giant industrial company we know today, he insisted on daily sales figures gathered from dealers around the country. There were no modems and no faxes in those days: clerks received the figures by phone and mail. Today, remote PCs transmit figures automatically each evening to the head office computer.

Some 100 million personal computers (*including Apple/Macs*) are in use worldwide, with close to 85% of them using Microsoft's *DOS* Operating System. About 10% are Macs and the remainder use more powerful operating systems designed for workstations.

Summary of the FRESHMAN Chapter

☐   A *Computer* is a <u>*machine*</u> that follows instructions (software) to perform tasks.

☐   <u>*Hardware*</u> is the parts we can see or touch, whereas <u>*Software*</u> is the instructions that reside in memory while the power is on.

☐   The <u>CPU</u> is the computer's *engine* or *brain*.   The CPU processes the software instructions retrieved from RAM line by line, and outputs the results back to RAM.   All the functions of the computer, are ultimately controlled by the Central Processing Unit.

☐   A <u>mouse</u> is a screen pointing device which reduces your use the keyboard.

☐   <u>Memory</u> is measured in *kilobytes* and *megabytes*.

<u>PC Warning:</u>   The Surgeon General has figured out that PCs can be *addictive*.   Persons using their PC for 600 hours per month shall be treated as *Nerds* in need of rehabilitative care.

Further Study

Page #:	Notes:
	☐
	☐
	☐
	☐
	☐
	☐
	☐
	☐
	☐
	☐
	☐

Terms to Learn	

... the INDEX starts on page 199.

SOPHOMORE

> **Computer Categories**

What separates PCs from other computers is that they are designed to be used by just one person. Originally most computers were *multi-user* systems, which allow hundreds of terminals (users) to access a single computer. It wasn't long, however, before *PC* users wanted some of those **mainframe** features like magnetic **disk** storage and sharing files ... high density diskettes, fast hard disks and **networks** were developed in response.

A mainframe is the largest of the **multi-user** computers and was popularized around the world most successfully by IBM. It is typically used by large corporations, government agencies, universities, and the military.

Recent advances in the PC field have resulted in a new sub-category being added, resulting in a blurring of the distinction between PC (micro) and Mini computers. This new sub-category is called a "*workstation*" or "*supermicro*". It has the extra processing power and **multitasking** capability for engineering work (**CAD**) previously found only in mainframes.

⬛➡ **Third Generation Computers are generally divided into four categories:**

① **Micro** _____ 🖳 Personal Computers and Workstations ($500 - $25,000). Made possible by the new technology of Integrated Circuits (**IC**s), which enabled mass production of low-cost *microprocessors* beginning in 1971.

② **Mini** _____ 🖳 Multi-user, medium sized capacity ($25,000-$750,000). Developed in the 1960s as a scaled-down **mainframe** to enable medium-sized businesses to utilize computers.

③ **Mainframe** ___ 🖥 Multi-user, very fast with the ability to process enormous amounts of data: large companies and government ($750,000+). This was the first of the modern (1950s) computers and the basis of *IBM's* prosperity. Banks, most large businesses, universities, government agencies and the military are the main users.

④ **Super** _____ 🖥 ⬛➡ The fastest and most expensive. Special use: military, a few universities and hi-tech research groups are the only users who can afford these *roadrunners* ... *beep beep!* These will be covered in more detail in the last chapter as a special interest item.

➤ What's a Nanosecond? ⌛

Because we are dealing with such minute slices of time in computer circuits, fractions of a second are used to measure time. Thousandths are expressed as *milliseconds*, and billionths as *nanoseconds*. The Latin word for thousand is *mille*, hence a *millimeter* is one thousandth of a meter.

You can visualize a *nanosecond* this way: In theory an electric signal will travel through 186,000 miles of wire in just one second (the speed of light). That's New York to LA and back almost 70 times in just one second! In one billionth of a second, or a *nanosecond*, it will travel almost one foot. In a typical 0.6"x0.6" *chip*, you can understand why the signals take a negligible amount of time to get around.

It's only when the distances are intergalactic that we can begin to appreciate the speed at which light travels. In the vacuum of space it takes about 8 minutes for the Sun's rays to travel to us, and a little closer to home, about 1.3 seconds before we see reflected light from the Moon.

➤ What's the advantage of a Digital Computer?

Computers are digital because they work in *digital* values of *zeros* and *ones*. The word we so commonly use, but give little thought to, is derived from the word "digit" which means, any of the 10 Arabic figures we use as numbers (0-9). A computer can be either *analog* (*speedometer*) or *digital*. An example is found in the two most popular watch faces. The older type with continuously moving hands is *analog* ☾, whereas the newer display with the time in numbers is (09:30:13), of course, *digital*. Time is a continuous measure, most correctly expressed by a *analog* clock face with a second hand.

Computer languages use *zeros* and *ones* to represent the *On/Off* status of its circuits. These two numbers are used to represent the absolute choices: Yes/No, True/False, which become *On/Off* instructions to a computer. Digital information can be expressed using a tiny fraction of the data it would take to describe a situation with variables.

The world we live in, and more particularly, the world we see and hear, is a continuous rhythm of information, described as *analog*. In comparison, when we see a movie, we are watching a series of individual frames, each with a tiny variation, which we perceive as normal motion. One second of real motion is divided into 24 discrete pictures, captured on film. In real life, that same scene is sent to our brain from the eyes as a continuous stream of imagery.  The 24 snapshots are sufficient for us to *perceive* it as analog information. Engineers worked out the *minimum* number of still pictures we need to see in a second, to *perceive* normal animation, thus saving a great deal of film. Likewise, there is less sound data in a digital CD recording, than we would hear in a live symphonic performance, but can you hear the difference? Digital music, such as we hear on a CD, is actually a series of discrete notes, so that we *hear* it as continuous, or analog sound. The hoopla about *digital* recordings lies in the abilty to record massive amounts of music onto a small disc, and to provide <u>unlimited replays</u> without perceivable errors (scratches, hiss, etc.).

In electronics, especially radio and fax transmission, error checking is vital. Discrete pieces of data, that is numbers, can be easily verified as being correctly received, a daunting task for analog data. Pictures from space probes are sent to Earth in a digital form, and although they suffer degradation through radio interference, the computer is able to reconstruct the images through *digital* error checking.

➤ What makes computers so Fast?

Computers are extremely fast because the signals flash through the circuits at _93,000 miles per second_, or half the _speed of light_. Secondly, with the exception of the Disk Drives, there are no moving or mechanical parts: it's all _solid state_. Thirdly, because Integrated Circuits (IC) are so tiny, the signals race very short distances. The _i486_ and _Pentium_ have the **coprocessor** built into the CPU to further reduce this distance. Signals inside the CPU however, travel at one tenth to one half of the _speed of light_ due to the resistance of the tiny wires and the insulating material around the wires. Outside the CPU these signals travel at about half the _speed of light_. Even so, the speeds involved are incredible!

In the never ending quest to reduce the time it takes for a signal to travel through the computer's circuits it is necessary to reduce the resistance and shorten the distance traveled. To reduce the effects of resistance we can use a lower voltage: it was 5 volts and the _Pentium_ is 3.3

volts, with 1 volt looming in the future. The insulating material, while necessary, is the big slowdown, as the signal travels on the surface of the wire, next to the insulator. **IC**s and tiny microprocessors solve the distance problem by making the distances traveled very minute. Indeed, compared with the older relay or vacuum tube computers which were connected by hundreds of miles of wire, signal distances are almost negligible.

Faster **clock speeds** (**MHz**) means switching the circuits on and off millions of times a second and that generates a lot of heat, hence the necessity for two fans in some PCs.

The time it takes for signals sent to RAM and the Hard Disk is also used to measure the computer's performance: the *Average Access Time* (also called *seek time*) of the RAM memory chips and the Disk drive. Memory chips are very fast and are normally measured in *nanoseconds* (50-120ns), while the slower Hard Disk and removable diskette drives are measured in *milliseconds*: 12 to 20 milliseconds (ms) for the Hard Disk and over 100 ms for the diskette drive.

➤ What does the Operating System do? ⌨🖱⇔💻⇔💾

Imagine you are taking tennis lessons ... you begin the lesson by picking up your racket ...

but wait, how did you know how to *operate* your arm? You coordinated eyes, arm, hand and fingers to pick up and grip the racket, without giving it a thought. We have a basic *operating system* which controls all the motor functions of our body ... it functions seamlessly in the background.

A computer's *Operating System* is similar. It is the underlying and essential *software* of every computer. It manages the operations between the program you are running, and the various parts of the computer, such as the CPU (Central Processing Unit), screen, keyboard, disk drives, and printer. In human terms it gives the computer consciousness or the awareness of itself.

The application program depends on the *operating system* to perform all the tasks associated with the otherwise invisible internal workings of the computer. The core of the *Operating System* resides in **RAM** memory while the computer is turned on, and additional functions that are used infrequently, are accessed on an as needed basis, from the disk.

DOS is an acronym for *Disk Operating System*, and in general usage *DOS* has come to mean *MS-DOS* (Microsoft's version) or *PC-DOS* (IBM's version), but it is a generic term applying to all operating systems that are disk-based. MS is an abbreviation for the developer, Microsoft Corporation.

MS-DOS is by far the most widely used operating system but it was designed with a 1970s model (64KB) *PC* in mind. It was selected by *IBM* for their *Personal Computer* in 1981, and to date over 100 million copies have been sold. *DOS* runs on the int**e**l family of microprocessors. UNIX is another, and *OS/2* (Operating System/2) which was developed to succeed *DOS*, is a later and more powerful system. *Macintosh* computers use a different Operating System, the latest being *System 7.5*, designed for the **Motorola** microprocessor.

➤ What is Windows?

MS-Windows is the world's most popular graphical operating system for the IBM compatible PC. IBM's *OS/2* is superior in many ways, but it has not been able to compete with Windows enormous popularity ...

Let's say *Windows* is like a dollhouse with a number of rooms, each with a different use (application). It has a kitchen, dining room, bedrooms, and finally a junk room. We can see into the dollhouse through openings or *windows*, and observe the furnishings and therefore the use of that room. In a similar way the software program called *Windows* allows us to divide up various computer tasks and move between them in a fast, but orderly manner.

Windows assigns each room, in computerese an *application*, a symbol or little icon. We are all familiar with the use of *symbols* at airports, and along the roadside: Recognition of a symbol is faster than reading words on a sign. Computer lingo, on the other hand, is as understandable as words found on rest room doors at foreign airports. We remember images better than words, like a persons face, but maybe not a name. The *Windows operating system*, which runs in conjunction with Microsoft *DOS*, brings this symbol system to the world of PCs. It's Microsoft's answer to *Apple's* fabulous operating system to which *Macintosh* users have long been accustomed.

Symbols, or icons as they are called, replace word commands on the screen, allowing the user to *point-and-click* with a *mouse* to perform many functions such as starting an **application** program, saving, copying or printing a file, and *cut-and-paste* functions. The very fact that it needs DOS is its main drawback, since the user must still face the *"C"* prompt at times.

```
1:*C:\WINDOWS\SMARTDRV.EXE  2048 2048
2: echo on
3: PROMPT ($p)
4: PATH E:\WINWORD;C:\;C:\DOS;
C:\WINDOWS;C:\UTILITY\XTREE;
C:\UTILITY\NORTON;C:\PCLINK
6: set mouse=C:\MOUSE
7: loadhigh C:\WINDOWS\mouse.COM /Y
8: PAUSE
9: SET NU=C:\utility\norton
10: IMAGE
11: set TEMP=C:\WINDOWS\TEMP
12: COPY C:\WINDOWS\PSPREP3.TXT LPT1
13: DEL C:\WINDOWS\TEMP\*.TMP
14: CHKDSK C: /f
15: Rem "Adding 'space/colon' to WIN
command deletes Start-up screen."
16: CD\WINDOWS
17: WIN
```

Does this look like *gibberish* to you? It's part of the DOS Autoexec.Bat file which runs each time the computer is turned on. Looks *messy* doesn't it? Well, *Windows* is designed to bypass *typed commands* and replace them with an *icon*. Double-click with the mouse arrow pointed to the icon and the computer loads the *gibberish* (instructions) into RAM ... nice huh? The Apple world has enjoyed this

ouble-click the Mouse on the icon.

system for many years, but eventually even *Big Blue* catches on.

➡   *Windows* advanced memory management breaks the DOS memory barrier of 640KB, allowing up to 16 **MB** of RAM to be addressed. It allows even more memory to be created by the use of ***Virtual*** memory. It also allows the computer to ***multitask***, that is to print, repaginate or recalculate in the background, while still running the current application in the foreground (more on that later).

➡ Its screen presentation of all *Windows*-supported applications is an accurate preview of the printed image you will see, known as *what-you-see-is-what-you-get* (WYSIWYG).

➡ It allows non-*Windows* applications such as *"1-2-3 for DOS"* to run in extended memory above the 640 KB *DOS* barrier.

➡ It provides a system for linking and transferring data between applications known as Dynamic Data Exchange (**DDE**).

Why not just throw out DOS and start again? That was the plan when IBM and Microsoft began work on OS/2; however, OS/2 requires a larger amount of RAM to function and it lacks 100% compatibility with popular application programs. Microsoft pulled out of the OS/2 program and pursued *Windows* ... With 80 million DOS users voting it's hard to make a radical change ... so *Windows* offers a transitional or gradual change. In the future *Windows* and *DOS* may be bundled together as one integrated, graphical, multitasking, operating system. *Windows NT* (*New Technology*) is Microsoft's high-end operating system designed for the server/network environment (it requires a *386/486* computer with a minimum of 8 megabytes of

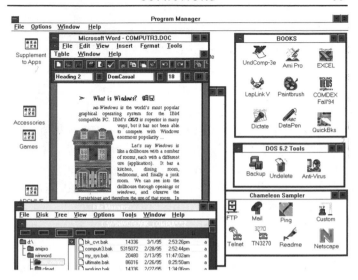

RAM versus 2 megabytes for *Windows 3.1*). It will compete head-to-head with IBM's OS/2.

Windows NT will have some stiff competition in the workstation market from NeXTStep, an advanced object-oriented operating system developed for the NeXT computer, and now available for the *486* platform. Beyond *Windows NT* Microsoft is working on *Cairo*, and IBM is working on *Taligent*, however these operating systems won't be available until 1996, at the earliest.

➤ What's Windows95?

It's the next version of *Microsoft-Windows* (after 3.1), which *was* scheduled for release in 1994. The release date has been postponed a few times as more conflicts (bugs) have been discovered. Commonly referred to as *Chicago* and *Windows4*, the official name *"Windows 95"* was announced at the Fall '94 **COMDEX**.

Microsoft wants to assert a break with the earlier versions of Windows, which operated in conjunction with DOS. As predicted, *Win95* will combine the whole operating system (*DOS & Windows*). It will be a major improvement over version 3.1 and offer many new capabilities, such as 32-bit power, while retaining backward 16-bit compatibility to run existing software apps:

✿ Other features include Microsoft's entry into the online service (via a modem) called "Microsoft Network" (MSN). Users will pay still a monthly fee after buying *Win95*, but will find "going online" a lot easier as it is fully integrated into *Win95*. *America Online, CompuServe* and *Prodigy* currently dominate this market.

✿ An old DOS barrier will be broken with full descriptive names for files and directories (now limited to 8 characters), and support for *Plug'nPlay* which allows easy hardware changes.

✿ A vastly improved File Manager called Explorer, plus context-sensitive help with a click of the right mouse button, *anywhere* on the screen.

✿ And best of all, "a driver's side air bag" for those terrible system lockups, aka *General Protection Faults*, which means when one app hangs you can still access the others. Only the most serious system conflicts should necessitate rebooting.

What's Bob?   In a nutshell it is a fun program to "make the computer easier to use" for the <u>home market</u>. [Technical jargon: "a better graphical interface"]. Yeah, yeah, you've heard that before, right? First time computer buyers may appreciate a "front door" to the computer that <u>doesn't come with a manual</u>, and in effect bypasses *Windows*! A typical household room scene appears on the screen: to start an application you click on a calendar, a piggy bank or a phone book, rather than choosing from a myriad of tiny icons. [*Bob* needs a 486 running at 50MHz or faster, with 8 megabytes of RAM].

➤ What's an Application Program?

When you sit down to write a letter you are *applying* yourself to a particular task. This is what application software does for the computer ... it enables the computer to perform a particular task. It is software written for a specific application or need.

These are some of the areas for which the most popular *application* programs have been written:

▦	Games
📄	Word Processing
📖	Desktop Publishing
▥	Spreadsheet/Graphics
▤	Accounting & Database

✦ Computer Aided Design (CAD)

If you want to write a letter on a computer, you need an [application] program designed to display text on the screen, and is able to perform such functions as *copying* and *moving* text. Routine typewriter functions such as tabs and carriage return, must also be included. Such an application program is known as a *Word Processor*.

If your need is to manipulate figures, you'll need a program that can understand formulas and does both simple and complex arithmetic. A *Spreadsheet* program would fulfill this requirement. Each of these broad areas (manipulating words and working with figures) is considered an individual application.

Processing data from satellites, high altitude baloons, and ground receiving stations, requires a different application program designed to interpret the measurements and come up with predictions for tomorrow's weather.

➤ What is Multimedia?

It's like *mass media* ... where we receive information in various formats: visual (TV), sound (radio), and text (print). *Multi* is the Latin word for *many*, and this new application software brings together the *many* ways in which we receive information ... by integrating video animation, sound, and photo-quality images with regular text and graphics on a personal computer. Beethoven's *Ninth Symphony*, the world *Atlas*, interactive tutorials, and full color encyclopedias with examples in motion, are examples of just some of the CD-based *multimedia* software available now. *Multimedia* is normally accessed from special CDs operating in a CD-ROM drive.

Multimedia has practical business applications, such as training and presentations. A person can learn much faster from an interactive video tutorial, than from a boring 100-page manual. Similarly, business presentations will benefit from animated color presentations with sound which now cost tens of thousands of dollars to produce.

Multimedia presents considerable technical problems because video images require massive amounts of storage compared with alphanumeric data (A, b, 1, 2), especially when motion pictures are combined with sound. Further, it requires a very high rate of data transfer from the storage medium, such as a laser disk. Laser or optical disks (music *CDs*) can store massive amounts of data but are slow in retrieving it compared to a magnetic disk.

Motion video such as we see on TV requires 720 kilobytes (KB) per frame of data be displayed at 30 frames per second. This means that one second of *digitized* video consumes 22.1 megabytes (MB) of storage. A standard CD-ROM with 648 MB capacity could hold only 30 seconds of uncompressed video! Further, because the data transfer rate is only 150 KB per second, it would take 5 seconds to display a single video frame!

The solution came with the introduction of the intel's *Digital Video Interactive* (DVI) board, which is a combination of hardware and software. By ignoring data that doesn't change in successive frames, DVI can compress data in video images by 20 times. In playback mode, it decompresses digital pictures and sound in real time. It is planned that by the end of the decade DVI will be included on the CPU.

➤ What's a Spreadsheet?

The name is a shortened form of *spreading the figures out on a sheet of paper*. In the early days of PCs a few software geniuses decided to computerize this very old paper system. The most common form of tabulating figures in business was by use of a ledger-sized (11"x17") sheet of paper divided into 14 columns, and about 30 rows. The first column listed the categories of income/expense items, followed by a column for each month, and finally a total column.

What makes a computerized spreadsheet so great? Once the numerical data has been entered into the computer, say a column of expense figures, a formula is placed at the bottom of the column to do the addition. That saves one error-prone step, however, there's much more. Let's say one of those expense figures needs to be changed ... by entering the new figure in place of the existing one, the formulae at the bottom of the column automatically recalculates the new total.

Quarterly BUDGET

	Jan	Feb	Mar	Total
Rent/Mortgage	780	780	780	2,340
Food	250	225	225	700
Utilities	125	95	75	295
Auto	50	75	125	250
Insurance	45	0	0	45
Total =	1,250	1,175	1,205	$3,630

Unlike its paper forebear, an electronic spreadsheet has hundreds of columns and thousands of rows. This allows the user great flexibility in laying out his work or simply positioning a table of figures in the spreadsheet. Each cell in the matrix or array created by the column/row format can contain either text, numbers or formulas. Rarely are all the cells in a spreadsheet used. The size of RAM memory is usually the limiting factor.

Its most important use, after simply tabulating numbers automatically, is the ability to do *what-if* scenarios. By changing one figure upon which other figures are linked by formulae, a whole new set of results can be instantly calculated.

When a figure is changed in a spreadsheet involving related formulae, the computer recalculates the solution for every formula in the spreadsheet. Normally this takes only a second or two; however, in a very large and complex spreadsheet involving hundreds of formulae, this recalculation time can lengthen considerably and therefore become annoying (early *programs* could not perform another function while it was recalculating).

Figures alone don't always convey information as well as graphics, and so spreadsheets also have the ability to portray a table of figures in a variety of graph forms such as pie, bar, and 3-D.

History: *VisiCalc* and *SuperCalc* were the first successful electronic spreadsheets, but due to the memory limitations of early computers, such computerized spreadsheets were often not much larger than their paper counterpart. In 1982 *Lotus* came out with an improved spreadsheet, named *1-2-3*, which was an instant success and propelled *Lotus* to become the number one software company in the world (*Microsoft* now has that title)! Millions of these programs (from different software companies) have been sold worldwide,

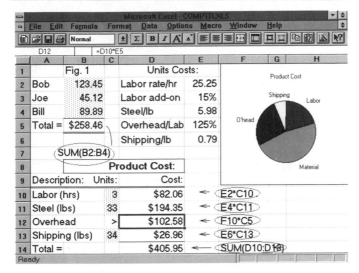

making it the second most widely used *PC*
application program.

The most popular uses for the spreadsheet
application are:

⊕ *What-If*
⊕ Budgeting
⊕ Product Costing
⊕ Cash flow analysis
⊕ Income and Expense analysis
⊕ Tabulation of scientific results

The leading *Windows*-based spreadsheets
are: *1-2-3, Excel, Quattro* and *Improv*.

➤ What's a Word Processor? ✍

What the automobile is to the horse and
cart the *word processor* is to the typewriter. A

word processor is a highly specialized software program that combines the features of a typewriter and a computer. This offers many advantages in addition to speed, including the ability to draft *soft* versions on screen, make corrections invisibly, revise documents on screen, rearrange and swap paragraphs between documents print multiple originals or multiple versions with minor variations, and store documents permanently on magnetic disk.

A *word processor* called *Word for Windows 2.0* (by Microsoft) was used to write this book. The screen *snapshot* (capture) shows how it looks on the computer screen.

Most word processing programs today include two very useful features: a *Spell Checker* and a *Thesaurus*. Some are also capable of checking grammar and sentence formation, though they will not turn gibberish into prose. **Typefaces** and font sizes can be varied on screen, along with traditional bolding, underlining, double-spacing and *italics*.

The legal profession was the first to see the potential for productivity improvement in using computers to generate their correspondence. Initially *Wang* dominated this market with **mini** computers; however, the real revolution came with the introduction of *PC*-based software such as *WordStar, WordPerfect*, and Microsoft *Word*. W*ord processing* is the most widely used *PC* **application**.

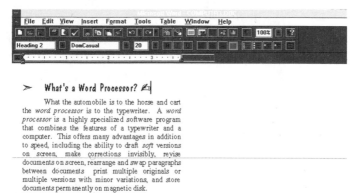

◼➡   **Features of a word processor:**

Word wrap automatically finishes a word on one line and flows onto the next line according to the margin setting, without use of the carriage return key.

Insert and delete text while the document automatically expands or contracts the surrounding text.

Cut, paste or copy text that allows easy movement and duplication without retyping. ✂

Page size and margins can be changed and the document will automatically reposition the text.

Search and replace allows the user to find any word or phrase without reading through the text.

WordPerfect for DOS still dominates in the legal profession; however, the *WYSIWYG* (*what-you-see-is-what-you-get*) power of *Windows*-based word processors, such as *Word for Windows* (Microsoft), *Ami Pro* (Lotus) and *WordPerfect for Windows*, are fast becoming the standard.

You don't need a PC just to write letters: A memory typewriter, such as Canon's model with ink-jet printing, should be considered for small writing projects, as they are portable and cost just a few hundred dollars.

The history of *Word Processing* can be traced back to ancient Egyptian scribes using *papyrus*, from which we derive the word *paper*. Such scribes could be likened to a modern day stenographer. In modern times it passes from devoted monks laboriously making handwritten copies of sacred writings, to the Gutenberg press of 1456, to the Lithography (literally *stone writing*) press of 1796. The typewriter which was invented in the early 1800s finally became a standard piece of office equipment by the early 1900s. The office duplicator and the Xerox copier which appeared in the '60s, while not able to generate originals, greatly facilitated the secondary requirement: fast, inexpensive copies. Finally today's *[word processing] PC* and printer, are the culmination of these prior developments in technology.

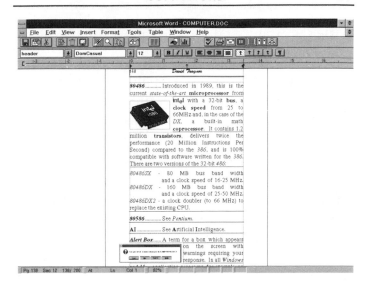

> ## What is Desktop Publishing? 📖

Desktop Publishing is all those steps involved in the process of producing a newsletter, a magazine, or a book, with a personal computer. *Desktop Publishing* starts where word processing stops, as it allows manipulation of the layout or the placement of text and images (such as pictures) on a page.

Aldus Corporation started the *Desktop Publishing* era with a program called *PageMaker* for the *Apple Macintosh* computer in 1985. The *Windows* version of *PageMaker* (for the IBM) was released two years later, in 1987. Such programs allow a personal computer and laser printer on one desktop to do tasks that had previously taken an art department, a typesetter, a paste-up expert, and a professional printer, hence the expression *desktop*!

Most professionally published documents such as newsletters, magazines and company reports include graphics, such as charts, pictures and logos; however, mixing graphics with text on a *PC* was very clumsy before this program came along. With a high resolution screen (e.g. **VGA**), the layout work can be performed on the screen before printing a hard copy, utilizing the *what-you-see-is-what-you-get* approach. A professional looking document can now be produced internally in a fraction of the time.

Desktop Publishing programs normally treat each page as a virtual document, allowing complete control over the placement of everything on the page. The distinction between desktop publishing programs and word processors is now being blurred, as the top-line word processors such as Microsoft's *Word for Windows* and particularly Lotus *Ami Pro*, offer most of the low and medium level features found in *desktop publishing* programs.

➤ What's a Database?

It's an organized mass of information (data) from which useful information can be extracted. Imagine a telephone directory that is not alphabetical ... it would be useless, right? If, however, we list the family names alphabetically, we have a useful base of information from which

we can derive phone numbers and addresses, correctly associated with those families.

Our phone directories are thick books; however, they are small *extracts* from the phone company's computerized *database* of its customers. The phone company also sells a *reverse* directory in which entries are listed by *address* (city, street, number, family name, phone number). Real estate sales people, among others, use this to find out who lives in a particular house. Extracting information in differing forms is easy when you have a computer database. By defining filters or criteria, it is possible to extract just the people who live in particular zip code, city or all the people who live on a particular street.

You've heard of the *Information Age* ... well, a computerized base of data (information), is the foundation. Imagine trying to look up all the President's speeches on the *National Debt* in just your own city's newspaper. A computerized index can search the matching subject references in **all** the libraries indexed publications (newspapers, periodicals, briefs) in about 30 seconds. This search will produce a list of the articles to research.

In the world of computers there are two different types of Databases: *Hierarchical* and *Relational*.

A **Hierarchical** database (also called a *flat database)* organizes data in a simple increasing or decreasing hierarchical order, of A to Z, or 0 to 100 (a phone directory is a good example). A *spreadsheet* containing sales data by area, salesman and month is an example of a simple database.

A **Relational** database is generally what people are referring to when speaking of a computerized database, as it is far more powerful in its ability to extract associated information. A *Relational* database is a group of two or more data files linked by a common denominator, such as a customer number. Rather than repeating the name, address, phone number and customer number in every file, a relational database keeps a separate file for address, sales and product information.

The sales file can draw on each of these by a common link, such as the customer number, each time the address information is needed. This not only reduces file sizes, but more importantly, it greatly increases the retrieval speed each time we access sales or other information on a customer. An accounting software program is basically a relational database designed for a specific purpose: a double-entry ledger system.

Summary of basic Database terms:

File _____ A *File* contains many records, perhaps thousands or even millions, in an organized manner. An example would be a computerized version of the phone directory.

Record ___ All the *associated* information in a *file* (e.g., name, address, phone, etc.), is one *record*.

Field _____ This is the building block of a database. For example, the last name and first name, within one *record*, would be two fields.

Summary of the SOPHOMORE Chapter

☐ A PC is based on a *microprocessor*, and is designed for use by one person.

☐ The Operating System is the underlying software that controls the computer hardware.

☐ *Windows* is a graphical Operating System that runs on top of DOS. It gives the IBM compatible the same graphical user interface as the *Mac*.

☐ Software programs which "do something" for us are called *Application* programs. The popular application types are word processing, spreadsheet, database and desktop publishing.

☞ **Bold face terms** are cross-referenced. The Index lists all the pages where they can be found, and the Terminology section gives detailed explanations of important terms.

There are approximately 75 million PCs and 21 million laser printers in use in the US.

... I'd rather know how many calories are in a cookie.

🖥

The COMPUTER industry is now the third largest industry in the USA, after Autos and Oil.

... when will it be #1?

🖥

The US Government is the largest purchaser of computers in the world.

... yeah, and guess whose money they're spending.

Now I understand the little fella ...

➤ Understanding Memory

A computer has two types of memory: one **temporary** *and the other* **permanent**. *The equivalent for us is what we retain in short-term memory, and what we keep as written records.*

❶ **Temporary Memory: RAM**   The computer's *temporary workspace,* is called RAM; it can be likened to an office desktop. It is *temporary* for two reasons:

1) Data stored in temporary memory is *volatile*, meaning it is lost when the power is turned off.

2) Changes you make *overwrites* the existing data.

     The CPU processes the **application** instructions and user data retrieved from RAM, and returns the results to RAM. RAM is an acronym for **R**andom **A**ccess Memory, which is the engineers way of saying any location (called a *register*) in RAM can be located by the CPU as quickly as another (random). RAM memory is located inside the computer on the **motherboard**, in the form of plug-in *memory chips*. Each memory **chip** can be likened to a wall of mail

boxes found at the Post Office, where each box, equivalent to a register, is either empty or has a letter in it. Each memory chip holds the equivalent of hundreds of thousands of such mailboxes ✉ ✉ ✉ ✉ ✉ ✉ ✉ ✉ ✉.

RAM capacity is measured in *Kilobytes* (KB) or *Megabytes* (MB), and it is the amount of RAM that determines how big an **application** program the computer can run, how big the user file can be, and how many functions the CPU can handle. It is generally possible to increase the amount of RAM in increments of the older 256 kilobyte or newer 1, 4 or 16 megabyte *chips*. The more demanding applications (parlance for memory hungry), such as desktop publishing and **multimedia**, require more RAM. RAM *chips* are considerably more expensive per megabyte than magnetic storage disks, so only portions of the application is held in RAM: the rest is swapped back and forth as needed.

RAM speed is measured in *nanoseconds* and is typically 50-120 nanoseconds. The computer's CPU and RAM are constantly exchanging data, so fast RAM chips are critical to the performance of the computer. The nanosecond rating measures how quickly data is *given up* by the chip, and how fast data can be *written to* the chip, as it is exchanged back and forth.

All the software instructions the computer needs to operate are normally *held* in RAM. This starts with the Operating System (*DOS* or *Mac System 7*), your application program (e.g. *Lotus 1-2-3* or *Word*), and any *Memory Resident* (**TSR**) applications automatically loaded (e.g. mouse driver).

To find out how much (RAM) memory your computer has, consult the manual, or try typing **MEM** at the DOS prompt: **C:** <u>mem</u> ↵

4. User File
3. Application
2. PopUp (TSR)
1. Operating System
RAM Chip

R_AM Burger

All the data in RAM is lost when the power is turned off for the day, or anytime power is unexpectedly lost. The remedy for unexpected power loss is buying a **UPS**, or frequent *saves* to the Hard Disk of your work (<u>if power is lost during a *save*, the file being saved to the disk(ette) will be corrupted</u>).

RAM memory chips have two main elements: transistors and capacitors. **Transistors** act as gates or switches, allowing new data to enter an address. Capacitors hold the data in the form of a charge (representing a 1), or the absence of a charge (representing a 0). Memory chips are divided into individual areas or addresses which can be likened to mailboxes 📪 📭 referred to earlier. A matrix of columns and rows, much like the map coordinates of a street directory, allows the CPU to find its way around all the address locations where each piece of data is stored. The CPU controls the storing and retrieval of the data stored in RAM. (A more detailed explanation of transistors is provided in the **Terminology** section).

Many businesses purchase a separate piece of equipment known as a *UPS*, or Uninterruptible Power Supply. This electronic device is about the size of a shoe box and contains a micro sensing circuit, a nicad or lead-acid battery, an inverter (DC to AC), and a trickle charger. The UPS is plugged into the power outlet and the computer into the UPS. Anytime it detects a loss of power it *kicks in* by inverting the DC battery voltage into 110 volts AC instantly, thereby preventing loss of RAM data, or damage while the disk is saving. APC (800/800-4272) is highly recommended as they offer a range of budget and ti-tech UPSs.

❷ Permanent Memory: Disk This is the computer's *disk-based* memory, as data is stored magnetically on a coated disk. Unlike memory chips the disk does not need the power turned on to maintain stored data, but it does need power to access (read/write functions) the disk. The advantage to storing the data magnetically is that it can be erased, or overwritten, as new data is generated.

A 5¼" Floppy Disk
and a 3½" Diskette.

A disk may be either a permanent hard disk or a soft (*floppy*) diskette. *Hard Disks* are so-named because they are a series of 3½" metal disks inside a hermetically sealed (air/dust proof) box ... a miniature version of the old "*45" juke boxes*, complete with a pickup arm. The whole unit is known as a ***Hard Drive***. The similarity to a juke box is only in appearance since the metal disks are specially coated to allow millions of magnetic read/write activities. These disks spin at very high RPMs and the arm pivots back and forth but never touches the surface. If it does, you have a ***crash***, and this is normally catastrophic for the sensitive magnetic data.

The technology for storing magnetic data on a disk is very similar to the process used to store music on a cassette tape, except that music is stored in an analog form, and computer data is stored digitally as **binary** numbers. (Advanced digital music systems store the music as binary digits for a very exact reproduction with less chance for distortion.)

Another type of storage disk is the ***Optical Disk***. These work on the same principle as your *Compact Disk* player, which uses a laser beam to scan the digitally encoded surface. Most optical disks, unlike magnetic disks, are read-only, known as *WORM* drives (Write Once Read Many times); however, more expensive read/write laser drives are available. The advantage of laser optical disks is their very permanent data storage, meaning they are unaffected by stray magnetic fields, making them ideal for archive purposes. Secondly, they can store massive quantities of data per disk, enabling color photographs to be included. A color photo alone can take 1MB to digitally encode. The disadvantage compared to magnetic storage is that they are comparatively slow in accessing data.

Libraries use optical disks for information search databases. All the leading magazines' articles are indexed by subject and key words on disks, which are mailed out to subscribers monthly. Library users can then research massive quantities of current publications in about 5-10 seconds per search.

Another popular use of optical disks in the home and office is ***Multimedia*** information disks (text, diagrams, graphics, motion video, and sound). Whole encyclopedias with diagrams, libraries of music, reference books, financial data and other fascinating information can be accessed from an optical disk and a *PC*.

✹ NERD STUFF ✹

Early PCs had only 64KB of *Conventional* RAM, with a DOS imposed limit of 640KB. To break this DOS barrier various schemes were developed by the computer giants, notably *Lotus,* int$_e$l and *Microsoft (LIM)*.

RAM between 640 KB and 1 MB, known as "Upper Memory", is normally reserved for the computer and the video display, however DOS 5 and 6 can use this for certain purposes, such as loading **drivers**. Memory beyond 1MB may be configured as either *Extended* or *Expanded* memory depending on software requirements. *Expanded* memory was very popular among many older DOS programs; however, the trend is clearly towards *Extended*, with the widespread use of *Microsoft Windows*.

RAM can be increased by another type of memory known as ***Virtual Memory***. By swapping parts of an application program, and/or parts of your current file, between RAM and the Hard Disk, the computer is able to handle very large files, and even multiple applications (under *Windows, System 7, OS/2, and UNIX*). Some DOS application programs, and all *Windows* applications, take advantage of this.

The advantage of *Virtual Memory* is that it is easy to setup, it functions in the background, and there is no cost to add 10 megabytes to the computer's RAM memory! The disadvantage is that it is much slower than accessing data stored in RAM (120 **nanoseconds** versus 40 **milli**seconds), and it reserves a big chunk of your hard disk.

➤ What does the Disk do? [image]

It's the computer's version *of "pen and paper"*. A disk is the *permanent* (non-volatile) part of the computer's memory system. It keeps your work, the application programs, and the Operating System (*Windows/DOS, System7*) stored, like music on a casette tape, until you decide to change it. When the power is off, the data is safe, but to access or to change it (read/write), the power must be on. The computer's RAM memory can only hold the actual **application** program and your work: everything else must reside on a disk ready to be accessed. The computer's [temporary] RAM memory, is small by comparison, typically 2, 4 or 16 megabytes, compared to the Hard Disk's [permanent] capacity of 80 to 500 megabytes.

[image] ▭ There are two types of disks. A removable ***Diskette***, often referred to as a *Floppy Disk*, and an internal ***Hard Disk***. The *diskette* generally stores from 720 kilobytes to 1.4

megabytes of data, compared to a *Hard Disk*, which typically stores 40 to 300 megabytes. Capacity is not the only difference: the hard Disk drive is considerably faster in read/write activities, or retrieving and saving files. Disk drives are rated by their *average access time*, measured in milliseconds (12-40 msecs is typical).

The diskette drive is the primary drive as all programs must first enter the computer via this drive. Because of the diskette's limited storage and slow access, most systems add a Hard Disk Drive. Once the Operating System is stored in the  root directory (normally *C drive*), a computer can be *booted*, or started from the Hard Disk. Application programs and user files are also normally stored on the Hard Disk and accessed from there. From the Hard Disk, programs and files are loaded into RAM, where the CPU can perform the task we require.

➤ How does a Disk work?

A Disk's magnetically prepared surface records the binary data written to it by the disk drive *head*. As it does not need electricity to keep the data stored when the computer is turned off, it is considered permanent.

A Hard Disk is so-named because it is a metal disk. A diskette or *floppy disk* is made from a non-rigid material, usually mylar. Both disk surfaces are coated with metallic particles, normally iron oxide, which, in common parlance, is *rust*, hence the brown color of *floppy's* surface! Although very similar to the recording technique used on audio recording tape, a computer disk records only ones and zeros, by either magnetizing a particle (1) or leaving it alone (0). Each of the iron oxide particles on the disk is a tiny permanent magnet embedded in the resin so it cannot move. However, the particle's *magnetic direction* can be reversed by an external magnetic field, such as the read/write head of a disk drive.

Data stored magnetically on the surface is divided into concentric circles, called tracks, which are in turn divided into sectors. The spacing or closeness of these tracks determines the **TPI** (tracks per inch) rating, and therefore the capacity of the disk. The TPI is determined by a combination of the manufacturing process (surface quality) and the accuracy of the formatting (read/write head in the disk drive). A high density 3½" disk has a rating of 135 TPI.

➤ Why does a Disk have to be Formatted?

Formatting prepares the disk's surface for the structure of file storage which the computer's

Operating System (*DOS*, *System 7*) requires. It also determines the capacity of the disk (KiloBytes or MegaBytes). To copy or move files, both the removable diskette and the Hard Disk, must be formatted by the same or a compatible Operating System.

Formatting divides the surface of a disk into two main areas: the *system* area and the *data* area for storing programs and user files. The system area is further divided into three subdivisions: the boot record, the **FAT**, and the root directory. The system area contains all the necessary information for the save/retrieve activities, and while it occupies the first track, it's only a small portion of the disk's capacity.

> ## ➤ What is Disk Compression?

Even a 200 MB Hard Disk can *"bulge at the seams"* when a few Windows applications and lots of graphics and fonts are added. There is an alternative to replacing the Hard Drive or buying another ... it's an inexpensive software technology called *disk compression*. You may have noticed that most original program disks are in a compressed format. *Disk compression* can turn your 200-meg hard disk into a 300-meg in seconds, without slowing the access or retrieval time. The process is something like a stenographer's *shorthand*, only it uses mathematical algorithms to *compress* and *decompress* both graphics and text, ***on-the-fly***. The latest version of DOS includes compression utilities that can run from Windows, and there are a number of after market products that offer more features such as *Infinite Disk* from Chili Pepper Software (800) 395-1812.

➢ What are the parts of a Diskette?

Lay a 3½" diskette, or a 5¼" floppy disk, on a flat surface in front of you. The newer 3½" rigid diskette has a protective "sliding door" over the media surface which is automatically opened when you insert the diskette into the drive. Inside the protective jacket of both types of disks is a round piece of plastic (mylar) with an ultra-thin layer of magnetized iron particles on the surface.

The older 5¼" floppy has three cutouts in the protective jacket. The center one allows the disk drive motor to rotate the disk, and the elongated cutout closer to the edge gives the drive's read/write head access to the magnet surface (where the data is written). A small square "notch" is cut into the side of the protective jacket of a 5¼" floppy. If you cover this with some tape the data on the disk becomes "protected" from changes.

The 3½" and the 5¼" are not interchangeable. Each requires its own disk drive.

➤ Some of my diskettes have one hole in the corner and others have two ...

One hole means it is a low density, or 720kB diskette, and the second hole which is always open, indicates a high density (1.44MB or higher) diskette.

In the lower corner(s) of a 3½" diskette you'll see one, or two, square holes. If there is only one, it will look more like a square indentation. On the back side you can see a rectangular slot with the small black square covering half of the indentation. This is a sliding switch.

➤ What does the little switch on the back of my Diskette do?

On the front side of a 3½" diskette you'll see one, or two, square holes in the lower corner(s). Looking at the backside, you'll notice the lower right hole has a little sliding "switch" built in. The "switch" is operated by inserting your finger nail and gently sliding it to either side of it's rectangular slot. Don't leave it in the middle: slide it all the way. When the sliding switch covers the hole, the diskette can be "written to" by the disk drive. When it is "open" you can see through the little square hole and the data on the diskette cannot be changed. This is a nice feature when you want to prevent accidental "overwrites" such as putting the wrong diskette into the drive and saving (writing to) the diskette. There is no restriction in "reading" files from the disk; it simply prevents changes.

➤ Is there a correct way to apply Disk Labels?

Yes. The "correct" way is to apply the self-adhesive label so that the "Read/Write" words are next to the "switch" on the backside. The blank area of the label allows you to write information about the contents of the disk (subject, program name, date saved, owner's name, etc.). When disks are stored in a container place the read/write end in first so that it is away from your fingers.

The labels come in a variety of colors to assist you in labeling like-kind disks. (You could give backup disks a red label and tax data disks a green label, or Johnny's disks blue labels and Mary's ones red labels).

➤ Handling a Diskette?

Pick up the disk between your thumb and forefinger, and if it's the older floppy style, don't squeeze it. Locate the disk drive opening (the horizontal opening may appear closed) and insert the diskette gently with the read/write end first. Push the last half-inch or so, in with the tip of your finger. You should feel a mechanical click as grabs the diskette and automatically locks it in place inside the drive. The diskette is now ready for use. If it's new, it will need formatting (unless you purchased formatted disks). To remove the diskette push on the eject button, which is a part of the drive. **DO NOT eject a diskette when the drive is operating** - a little light on the drive illuminates when it is operating (laptops may have the "drive active" indicator somewhere else).

➤ Backups are Vital!

When the old-west Sheriff went out to meet the gunfighter, he usually had a *backup* gunman nearby. Modern aircraft have redundant, or *backup* systems, in the event the primary system fails. Hard Disks, like systems in an aircraft, are extremely reliable, however, *they do fail* ... it is therefore prudent to make daily *backups* of at least your working files. MS-DOS has a command called *Backup*, however, unlike *Copy*, files saved by this method can only be retrieved by using the *Restore* command.

The simplest and cheapest *backup* is to copy the files to a diskette, using the DOS *Copy* or *Backup* commands. Since diskettes only hold about 1.4 megabytes, that system has its limits.

Leaving aside the remote possibility of a Disk *crash*, one must also consider that PCs are a *hot* item to steal. Insured PCs can be replaced, but what about all your work stored on that little magnetic disk?

Another alternative is to install a tape backup system (internal or external). Removable hard disks offer the speed and reliability of a hard disk, with the ability to make multiple backups. The removable disks allow different people to use the same CPU (shifts) without using up the main Hard Disk. Multiple *backup* disks, tapes and cartridges should be kept at another location and rotated on a regular basis.

➤ Microfilm

Microfilming should not be overlooked as an inexpensive means of storing large quantities of business records. Microfilm bureaus are able to transfer data from diskettes directly to film, bypassing the labor intensive photographic operation. Microfilm can also be encoded for indexing, greatly speeding the search process. Offers greater reliability as magnetic disks can be erased by magnetic fields.

Libraries make great use of this technology, though it will be replaced gradually as the cost of *writable* CDs (650 megabytes) is declining rapidly.

➤ What is a Network? 🖥⇔🖥

Personal Computers, by definition, are normally stand-alone computers, but when *PCs* are joined together by a communication system (cable, radio or infrared), they are said to be *networked*. A network enables *PCs* to share programs, user files and peripherals (i.e., printers), and to emulate some of the capabilities of multi-user mainframe and minicomputers. Just as cars move safely back and forth on freeways, data moves in a similar way on a *network*.

In the context of *PCs*, it is usually called a *LAN* or Local Area Network. Different types of computers such as IBM compatible *PCs*, *Minis*, *Mainframes*, and *Apple Macintoshes* can all be a part of the same *network*.

Network PLUSes and MINUSes:

+ Ease of file transfer

+ Share expensive peripherals, i.e. printers

- Expensive to set up (boards, cabling & *server*)

- Maintenance of system

Sales information entered by the Accounting department can be accessed by an executive *PC* to generate the quarterly budget. Peripherals such as laser printers, scanners, and modems can be shared by different *PCs* thus maximizing their use. There are three popular network designs: Bus, Ring and Star.

In a *PC* network, multiple stand-alone computers and printers are linked together, allowing the sharing of peripheral equipment and data. When a file is being worked on by one computer, *"file locking"* prevents anyone else from accessing it at the same time. In a multi-user environment many terminals can access the same files and be adding and deleting to the file at the same time.

As an inexpensive, though not seamless alternative to networking, you might consider an inexpensive product named *LapLink*. Although it's designed to serve the needs of file transfers between desktops and portable PCs, any two PCs can easily be connected via their serial or parallel port with this product. Once connected, files can be transferred at the astounding rate of 3 megabytes per minute!

➢ What is the difference between Multi-User and Multitasking?

The term *Multi-user* can be likened to six hungry boys all diving into the same food bowl. Whereas *Multitasking* is like a busy mother who has something in the oven, is talking the kids, signing for a delivery and answering the phone.

Nearly all the computers (mini & mainframe) in use prior to the arrival of the PC were *Multi-user*, meaning two or more, even hundreds of terminals, can be entering and retrieving information from one computer. This is quite different from a *PC* which is designed to be used by only one person, performing one *task* at a time. Hence the term *Personal Computer*.

The MS-DOS Operating System was not designed to handle more than one user, and certainly *IBM* did not want *its PC* to compete with its line of very profitable large computers. It is the operating system, not the hardware, that determines whether a computer has *multi-user* capability.

The same *microprocessor* upon which a *PC* is based (e.g., *80486, Pentium*) can be used with a *multi-user* operating system (e.g., UNIX), to operate multiple *dumb* terminals (screen and keyboard only).

Multitasking is in effect when a *PC* is running two or more application programs concurrently. *Multitasking* allows you to start a complicated spreadsheet recalculation, put that in the background, then call up your personal appointment calendar, followed by drafting a letter with the word processor, and finally return to the spreadsheet which has finished recalculating along with sending your letter to the printer.

Multitasking holds each program in the computer's RAM *chips*, available for instant use. Without this capability DOS requires you to exit one program and then load the next one, a time-consuming task compared to switching between application programs. *Multitasking* is only practical on a faster *PC* such as the *386, 486 or Pentium*, with four to sixteen megabytes of RAM memory. MS-DOS on its own does not support *multitasking*; **Windows** and *Mac's System 7* supports limited *multitasking* (i.e., background printing). *WindowsNT* and *OS/2* offer a true *multitasking* operating environment.

How does it work? The CPU only processes one instruction at a time. However, it takes so little time to process each instruction that it appears to be doing them all at the same time. By a technique called *time-slicing*, the various tasks in a *multitasking* situation are divided, and each is given a *slice* of the CPU's time or clock cycles. Remember the clock speed (MHz rating - 16, 20, 33, 50 or 66) of the CPU ? ... that's *millions* of cycles per second.

✹ NERD STUFF ✹

➤ DOS vs. UNIX and OS/2.

MS-DOS was developed by Microsoft in 1981 as a *single-user* Operating System for the early PCs. UNIX was developed by *Bell Labs* in 1969 for the Minicomputer, and like *MS-DOS* it has gone through many revisions. UNIX (Xenix), unlike DOS, is a *multi-user*, *multitasking* Operating System. Like *Windows*, *OS/2* is also *multitasking*; however, its big feature is its graphical, or *object-oriented*, operating environment.

Both are more powerful and versatile than *MS-DOS*, but in the case of *OS/2*, it realistically needs at least a 386/33 computer with 8 megabytes of RAM and 15 to 30 megabytes of disk space. Graphical operating systems, such as *Windows* and *OS/2*, are easier to use but require a lot more RAM and a faster CPU to display and operate the impressive screen graphics, than plain old *DOS*.

It's easy in the *Mac* world as there is only a choice between earlier versions and the latest operating system, *System 7.5*.

Application programs are designed to function with a particular Operating System (*MS-DOS*, *System 7*, UNIX, OS/2), so an *MS-DOS* application program such as Lotus *1-2-3* or *WordPerfect* will not run on a UNIX based computer. Most off-the-shelf *PC* software is designed to run on *DOS*, and with 100 million copies sold, it is by far the most common operating system.

Many of DOS's limitations and most of its clumsiness have been remedied by adding Microsoft *Windows* which runs on top of DOS. It will operate on a one megabyte computer but prefers two or more megabytes of RAM to make it functional. It's *multitasking* and graphically based, giving it the look and feel of a *Mac*, without the memory overhead required by its more powerful rival, *OS/2*.

➤   What is Peripheral Equipment?

Any device (**hardware** equipment) that is outside the computer box but *connected to* the computer, and generally having little or no stand-alone function, is called a *peripheral* device. Some examples are a printer, plotter, external disk drive, modem, and a scanner.

➤   There must be a better way ...

to enter words and numbers into my PC without retyping it every time ... there is! You can *scan* data into your computer and even *talk* data into your PC.

➤   What is a Scanner?

It's a computer's version of a photocopier. Photographs, line art, and even text can be *scanned* so that the computer can store it, display

it on screen, and print the image. There are two types of scanners: *hand-held* and *flatbed*. The amateur *hand-held* unit is inexpensive and small (4" scanning width), with a resolution up 400 dpi (dots per inch). The more expensive professional *flatbed* unit scans a page at a time, is fast, easy to use, and offers high quality.

> *DataPen* by Primax is a pen-sized scanner which can read text, from tiny 8 points to heading-size 22 points. As you slide the scanner over the text, be it a newspaper ad, magazine article, financial report, or a fax letter, it converts the text to ASCII code and displays it on the screen. It's an ideal companion for a laptop, and takes little space beside a desktop PC (800) 774-6291.

Optical Character Recognition (OCR) programs can *recognize* typed letters on a sheet of paper and convert them into **ASCII** characters which a computer understands. Scanning text saves the enormous, and error prone effort, of retyping existing documents which we want to enter into the computer.

◎ What's Speech Recognition?

It's a technology that allows a PC to recognize *your speech* ... which means you can **TALK** to your computer! Finally, you can communicate with your computer in the same manner you communicate most of your thoughts ... *by speaking*. **Speech Recognition technology was used to make the revisions for this edition** (it's also known as *Voice Recognition*). Everything you presently enter via the keyboard, or with a mouse, can be accomplished with this exciting new technology. This wonderful technology opens up the world of PCs to many handicapped people.

The main players are *Dragon Systems*, which we use, and of course *IBM*, who has done a lot of pioneering work with this technology over the last twenty years, and *Kurzweil*. IBM's system is a little faster, but dictation appears in a special "speech window", whereas Dragon's version will work with any *Windows* software. It's present limitations are that it must learn each person's unique pronunciation, a pause must be added between word (discrete speech), and it's slower than normal dictation (about 40 words per minute).

Equipment? You'll need a high-end PC, such as a 486/66 with 16 MB of RAM and some room on your hard disk. The technology is mostly software, using the CPU to convert your speech into text and commands. You'll also need a sound card.

Dragon Systems (800) 825-5897; IBM (800) 825-5263; Kurzweil (800) 380-1234.

Inexpensive versions with a small vocabulary allow you to issue oral commands to the computer, such as "File Save", but not to dictate. These still need a sound card, but this is something many computers come with today, as it is used by **multimedia** CDs.

➤ Modems are for Communicating

A *modem* is a small gadget (in computer parlance a *device*) which allows two computers, in different locations, to *talk* to each other. A *Modem* is the computer's version of a FAX machine.

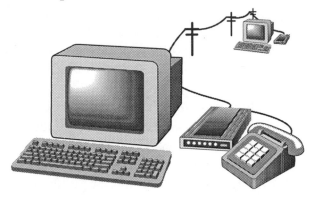

How does it work? When communicating via a telephone line, a modem converts (silent digital) computer language into sound (analog), and back into ones and zeros at the other end. This is known as **digital** to **analog** conversion. A modem allows a PC to *talk* to another computer anywhere in the world via a phone line, just as people can to each other. It doesn't have to be via a phone line, however, as other types of modems can *talk* to each other by radio waves or by infrared (like a TV remote), within a limited range.

When two computers are within cabling distance of each other a modem is not required. Many modern office buildings are being pre-wired with co-axial, or fiber optic cable, to allow

	Mail ✉	FAX/Modem ☽
Delivery Time ⧗ ⇨	1-3 business days ☹	1 minute ☺
Cost $ ⇨	32¢	10-25¢

easy computer communication within the building. A modem is not required if fiber optic phone cable is available, as this is a digital communication system. A modem can be either internal or external. An external modem is connected to a computer via a standard RS-232 port, usually located at the back of the computer box. An internal modem comes in the form of a modem board and is inserted into a vacant **slot** on the **motherboard**.

Modem communication speed is measured in **bits per** second (bps) and ranges from 2,400 bps to 28,800 **bps** rate. The bps rate is also referred to as the *Baud rate*. The rate of communication is determined by the slowest of the sending/receiving units. For an explanation of bits and bytes and related terms, refer to the Terminology and the Index sections.

WinFaxPro is a *Windows* application that allows paperless transmission of your faxes *directly* from the computer (via an internal or external fax/modem). Incoming faxes can be received and stored, and after conversion to **ASCII** text, faxes can be edited by your word processor! Faxes can be forwarded to another fax machine, or retrieved by your laptop when traveling.

Summary of the JUNIOR Chapter

☐ A *Computer* has *temporary* memory, called RAM, where it holds *work-in-progress*, and *permanent* Disk memory. RAM speed is measured in *nanoseconds* and the slower Disk Drives, in *milliseconds*.

☐ A disk's magnetic surface must be prepared, or *formatted*, before it can be used.

☐ PCs can *talk* to each other and share printers when they are *networked*. Networks can communicate via cable, radio or infrared.

☐ PCs are single-user, though they can perform multiple tasks simultaneously. The Operating System determines these attributes.

☐ A modem allows two distant computers to *talk* via a regular phone line.

☐ *Multimedia* offers a new way of communicating: animated images, sound and text!

☐ A *Backup* copy of your work is vital!

Don't give me that "file not found" rubbish!

☞ **Bold face terms** are cross-referenced. The **Index** lists all the pages where they can be found, and the **Terminology** section gives detailed explanations of important terms.

➢ **Apple or IBM and company?**

Apple / Mac

+ Graphical+Multitasking Operating System

+ Similarity between all applications

+ Network communication built-in

- Expensive (clones will sell for less)

- Difficulty exchanging files with non-Mac

- Only 10% of PC market worldwide.

IBM Compatibles

+ 90% of PCs worldwide

+ Inexpensive

+ Greatest choice in application software

+ Wide variety of competing equipment

+ *Windows* O/Sys + Application similarity

- Limitations of MS-DOS (memory, file names, etc.)

- Slower setup/learning curve.

➤ How much Memory do I need?

Like vacation money, more than you expect ...

❶ RAM Memory   Remember this is where the computer does its *work,* and to do any work it must first load the operating system (e.g. DOS/Windows) and **application** software (e.g. word processor) into RAM.   Next comes your work, that is (user files), or what you see on the screen.   *Windows* has greatly increased the demand for RAM, and newer graphical **applications** such as **Multimedia**, have increased this demand by *leaps and bounds*.   All of this is sometimes called "live data", as opposed to data permanently stored on a magnetic disk.   Without

 electricity flowing through the computer, it will lose the application along with your work, hence the expression *"live data"*.

RAM Burger

The original personal computers which appeared in the 1970s had 16 to 64KB of RAM.   When Bill Gates and company were writing the Disk Operating System (adopted by IBM for their *PC*), they decided that it should allow for expansion of the computer's RAM capacity.   He chose the extraordinary multiple of *ten times* the normal RAM size (at that time) as the upper limit of DOS.   For many years this kept the lid on the *PC*'s memory to 640 KB.

A typical *Windows* application program requires at least one megabyte of RAM to function. Don't forget, at least a portion of the operating system (e.g., DOS), and your work must also reside in RAM. The graphical screen presentations (as opposed to the old text messages) also increase the RAM memory requirements.

In summary, 1 MB (megabyte) is a minimum for today's computers, with 2 MB being a good starting point. The cost of memory chips continues to decrease, and adding more RAM as you need it is generally possible and inexpensive with most models.

❷ Hard Drive   The *PC* should be configured with more Hard Disk capacity than you think will be needed, normally a minimum of 100 megabytes. If you will be using a number of Windows applications, consider an 300MB drive or even larger, as the cost difference is not that significant.

This book, for example, contains about 185,000 characters or 37,000 words. In theory that means it will take 185 kB (kilobytes) of disk storage, right? In reality the file is over 5 megabytes of disk space! What's going on? The file includes quite a few graphics which are ravenous on memory, and a great deal of formatting code must be held with the text.

An application program such as Microsoft *Word for Windows* for example takes a minimum of 5.5 megabytes of Hard Disk space to a maximum of 14 megabytes, depending on how many options you install (clip art etc.).

Internal Hard Disk capacity ranges from 100 to 500+ megabytes and offers faster access time and greater reliability than the *floppy disk*.

After you use your computer for a while, you will be amazed at the number of files you create, and want to have available for ready access. To increase storage capacity, and build in redundancy, consider adding a second hard drive. Further information is located in the Terminology section under **IDE** and **SCSI**.

❸ Diskette Drive Data that is not currently in the computer's RAM memory can be accessed from a *Floppy Disk* or a **Hard Disk** Drive, which uses similar technology to the audio cassette tape.

The older style 5¼" *floppy* is rapidly being replaced with the 3½" rigid *diskette*. The 3½" diskette comes in 720 KB and 1.44 MB versions, with 2.88 MB and 4 MB drives as an option. Disks are inexpensive, easy to transport in person or by mail, and offer the possibility of making multiple backup copies. The 5¼" floppy disk comes in two versions which can store either 360 kilobytes or 1.2 megabytes of data. Early PCs had just a Disk Drive (no Hard Disk), hence the term DOS (**D**isk[-based] **O**perating **S**ystem.)

Backup copies of the Hard Disk, which are extremely important, can be made by using diskettes, an integral tape system, or various removable hard disk systems.

➤ What is a Coprocessor?

As the name implies it is a secondary processor which cooperates with the main processor or CPU.

While a computer does all its work or calculations in the central *processor* (CPU), it can do even faster calculations on numbers with the aid of a co-worker or *"co-processor"*. The most common type is a *math coprocessor* which handles the Floating Point Operations (measured in **FLOPS**). A math coprocessor allows math intensive calculations to be split off from the CPU and handled exclusively by the coprocessor, resulting in a much faster and more efficient computer. It is particularly suited for CAD operations. The *coprocessor* must be correctly matched to the central *processor* and be supported by the application software. intel makes three coprocessors for its line of processors: *80287* for the *80286* and the *80387* coprocessor for the *80386*. The intel *486* has a coprocessor built into the CPU. *Motorola* and *Wytek* also make a line of coprocessors.

A coprocessor will probably not improve the performance of the computer when it is functioning as a word processor, but may show a significant increase in performance recalculating a formula intensive spreadsheet, for instance.

➤ What does the BUS do?

The unseen internal communications of a computer travel via the computer's *bus*. If you think of computer as a small town, then the *bus* is equivalent to the town's road system.

Why should you care about Bus types? Performance. The primary factor in determining system performance is the CPU, however the *Bus* comes a close second. Driving a racing car on a jammed freeway would be the equivalent of a fast CPU communicating with the hard disk and other devices via a slow *bus*: the *bus* becomes the *bottleneck*. The bus design makes a *BIG* difference in speed - especially if you are using either graphic-intensive programs such as *Windows* or programs which make a lot of disk calls (e.g. database).

There are five competing *bus* types in use on IBM compatible computers: **ISA**, **EISA**, **MCA**, and two *LocalBus* designs. Macintoshes use another type, the *NuBus*. A table at the end of this section summarizes the differences.

The *bus* capacity or *width*, is expressed as being either 8-**bit**, 16-bit or 32-bit. This is analogous to the number of lanes on a freeway.

The more bits in the bus pathway, the faster the exchange of data and the faster the system speed as it is communicating in larger "chunks" of data. The computer *bus* is the pathway between the CPU and each device, such as the disk drives, the video display card, and the serial and parallel ports (for external devices-printer, etc.). The *bus* has a speed setting, analogous to the freeway speed limit. The older ISA *bus* runs at 8 MHz, and its successor EISA runs at 10 MHz. These speeds are all much slower than the 33-99 MHz clock speed of the CPU.

A revolutionary new type of motherboard, the *Local Bus* motherboard, is the latest *bus* contender in the designs for a faster PC. Graphically intensive applications such as *Windows* puts a strain on the PCs ability to rapidly display information, and while CPUs have quadrupled in speed, the bus design has not kept pace. It's like a city which has grown rapidly without the freeway system keeping pace. *Local Bus* offers much faster graphics performance by sending device requests directly to the CPU, thereby bypassing system bottlenecks, and by operating at the speed of the CPU itself (up to 33MHz). There are two contenders for *local bus* standards, the VESA[1] Local Bus (VLB) and the intel PCI (Peripheral Component Interconnect) standard. The VESA standard allows only three VLB slots and runs up to 33 MHz. The intel

---

[1] Video Electronics Standards Assoc., San Jose, CA

standard can have up to 10 *local bus* slots and runs at 33 MHz (on a 33 MHz computer). The VLB design has the rest of its slots in either ISA or EISA form. intel's PCI standard is considered more robust, and though behind VESA in its release, it will become the preferred *Local Bus* standard.

Using *Local Bus* can dramatically boost video performance and communications with the Hard Disk, on any 32-bit CPU such as the 386DX, *486*, or 64-bit *Pentium*. Future applications such as full-motion video, high-fidelity sound multitasking *Windows NT* will need *Local Bus* to perform acceptably.

A video accelerator card splits off the screen work to its own graphics co-processor (co-CPU) and RAM. A *Local Bus* system with an accelerated video card, and a *Local Bus* disk controller, can be 15 times faster! Avoid systems where the manufacturer has integrated a proprietary *local bus* video chip onto the motherboard: you can't choose, or upgrade with a standard plug-in accelerator board.

What happens when you press a key on the keyboard? ... Keyboard ➡ I/O ➡ CPU ➡ Bus ➡ Graphics Card ➡ Screen.

What happens when you save a file? ... I/O ➡ CPU ➡ RAM ➡ Disk.

BUS TYPE	YEAR	MHz and Bits per cycle	Transfer rate per second
ISA	1984	8 MHz 16	16MB
Macintosh NuBus	1987	20 or 30MHz 32	16MB
MCA	1988	10 MHz 32	40MB
EISA	1990	10 MHz 32	32MB
VESA Local Bus	1992	25 or 33MHz 32	133MB
PCI Local Bus	1993	25 or 33 32	120MB

➤ Designing a system ... the Hardware

Which computer is best for me?

USE	System Load	Apple Mac	IBM Compatible
Bookkeeping Word Processor	Low	Performa 475	486-25MHz
Spreadsheet	Med	575	486-33MHz
Desktop Publishing	High	Quadra 630	486-66MHz 586/Pentium
Multimedia	V.High	PowerPC	486/586
Network Server	V.High	PowerPC	486/586

If we compare a computer to an athlete, we can say the model is equivalent to the athlete's muscular development, the clock speed is analogous to his heart rate, and the bit rating is similar to his lungs in how fast it can pass oxygen into the bloodstream.

Here are some things to consider when you are designing your system ...

Microprocessor_____The single biggest factor in a computer system is the CPU model (*386, 486, Pentium/586*). The more powerful the CPU, the faster you see the results on screen. It's the computer's *"engine"*, and we all know a *Porsche* is faster than a *VW*. Some models feature an *upgradable* CPU socket (*or a Clock Doubler*) ... it is much cheaper to upgrade the CPU *chip* than to buy a new computer.

The correct matching of the following four factors determines the overall *speed* (instructions per second) rating of the microprocessor:

1. CPU model (*030,040; 386,486,Pentium*)
2. CPU clock speed (8-66 **MHz**)
3. Communication Bus (8, 16 or 32-**bit**)
4. RAM speed (40-120 **ns**) & amount.

Often the choice is limited to the first two items, however, by knowing all four factors you can better compare the price vs. performance between competing brands and models.

➤ The intel and *Motorola* family of microprocessors are described at the beginning of the Terminology section on page 145.

Clock Speed___ Each CPU model (*386, 486, Pentium, 030, 040*) has a particular *Clock Speed* measured in megahertz (MHz). A 66 MHz computer is roughly twice as fast as a 33 MHz model, in processing instructions. When a clock-doubler (see *OverDrive*) is plugged into the motherboard only the  CPU operations are accelerated; the RAM and bus operations on the motherboard remain at the pre-doubler MHz rating. The CPU internally executes instructions at either 8, 16, 32 or 64 *bits* per *clock cycle*.

Bus _____ A *wider* bus (bigger bit rating) can *gulp* more data on each cycle. Opt for the *LocalBus* design backed by intel, IBM, Compaq and NEC, known as **PCI**.

Monitor _____ There are choices in this area too, such as monochrome or color. The most popular standard is VGA while SuperVGA and now ExtendedVGA offer even greater picture quality. Large screen monitors are still pricey. The most important factor is the pitch of the screen pixels: 0.31mm is OK, but 0.28mm spacing gives a sharper image. The next is screen refresh as this is what we see as flickering. A refresh rate of 60 Hz (cycles/sec.) can cause eye fatigue, so look for at least 72Hz.

SCREEN	Year	Resolution	Colors
CGA	1981	320x200	4
EGA	1984	640x350	16
VGA	1987	640x480	256
8514/A	1987	1024x768	256
SVGA	1990	1024x768	256
XGA	1990	1024x768	65,536

A SVGA screen can display 768 rows, each with 1024 pixels across. A screen's size is measured diagonally (14", 17", etc.)

Keyboard _____ Now the choices are simpler. There are two keyboard designs to choose from ... Standard or Extended. The 101-key extended design has an additional number pad and scroll keys, so it is easier to use, but wider.

RAM _____ In general from two to ten **megabytes**. *Windows* applications need more RAM than the non-graphical (DOS) applications. Remember the size of RAM affects the computer's speed and ability to run multiple applications simultaneously (**multitasking**). Most systems make it easy to add more RAM to the motherboard; this is preferred to additional RAM on an expansion card. Refer back to **Memory** on pages 73 and 102.

Hard Disk ____ At least 40 megabytes, however if will be using *Windows* applications opt for at least a 100-megabyte drive as *Windows* applications use more disk space. If your files contain graphics or pictures they will take up much more disk space than text-only files. Refer back to **Memory** on pages 73 and 102.

Coprocessor ____ It depends on the application. Refer to **"What is a Coprocessor"** on page 105.

➤ Which Printer is right for me?

There are four types of *desktop printers*:

All four types of printers actually print with *dots*: the difference is the size of the dots, and how closely those dots are spaced (measured in dots-per-inch). Increasing the density of *dots* that are printed, improves the sharpness the text and images. Even the monitor uses *dots,* called *pixels,* to display an image on screen. A professionally printed glossy magazine is printed at 2450 dpi, compared to 1200 dpi for a high-end laser, but you would have to look closely to see the difference. Of the 12 million printers sold (in the US) in '94, 44% were ink-jets, 30% laser, 25% dot-matrix, and 1% were all other types including thermal transfer.

$$ ___ Ink-Jet - This category has tripled its share

of the printer market since '92. It can produce sharp *color* images and line drawings at 720 dpi (dots/inch) for a bargin price. Like the laser it is very quiet, though the color cartridges can be expensive. For very sharp color work, special paper is recommended. Like a laser, it uses sheets of paper (letter or legal). *Ink-jets* have taken the home market by storm with inexpensive, high-quality models, offered by Canon and Epson.

$$$ __ Laser - This category begins at under $500 for a 4-page per minute, non-color printer. The laser's output looks the best as it can print solid blacks, and complex fonts and graphics. The quality, or *blackness*, of its output remains consistent as it consumes the toner from the replaceable cartridge. Because a laser is a page-printer, it can do all this without sacrificing print speed. Lasers are fast,

quiet and offer resolutions of 300, 600 or 1200 dpi (dots/inch). Even at 300 dpi the laser's output is sharper than either the 360 dpi dot-matrix or ink-jet, because it uses smaller dots. The expensive professional lasers can print 1200 dpi on 11" x 17" paper allowing two 8½" x 11" documents to be printed on one page. The faster models (8-page/min.) are ideal for an office network, and the high-end color models are still very expensive, but produce dazzling color printouts and slides. The camera ready copy for this book was printed on an *HP LaserJet 4M* (600 dpi) using *Adobe PostScript* fonts.

$ ___ *Dot-Matrix*
- Though its output is not as snazzy, it is faster in black ink and the least expensive type of printer to operate (supplies). If you need to print *multipart forms*, you must use an impact printer. To print large spreadsheets on the ledger-sized (11"x17") paper, you'll need either a *wide-carriage* dot-matrix printer, a high-end *ink-jet*, or a very expensive laser printer. Something else to consider is that the print quality deteriorates gradually (gets lighter) over the life of the (ink-soaked) ribbon. Great improvements have been made in the infamous screeching sound of these printers, especially in the (slower) *quiet* mode. Speed is rated in characters per second (cps): 300cps is equivalent to a six page-per-minute (ppm) laser.

$$$ __ Thermal Transfer - Color quality is superb, and speed is OK with this technology. Fargo offers an excellent range at reasonable prices and LaserMaster offers an excellent poster-sized model.

Printer PLUSes and MINUSes ...

PRINTERS	Quality	Noise	Speed	Color
Ink-jet	High	Low	Slow-Med	Yes
Laser	Very High	Very Low	Fast	Pricey
Dot-matrix	Med-High	Med	Slow-Med	OK
Thermal trans	Very High	Very Low	Med	Yes

CD-ROM Drive A *Compact Disk - Read Only Memory Drive* can access a whopping 680 **megabytes** of information per disk. It is required if you want to utilize some of the newer software such as **multimedia**, which comes on CD disks. The CD-ROM drive is normally connected as an external **peripheral** device via one of the **ports**, allowing it to be used by different PCs.

➡*Software* Many software retailers have an on-site computer to demo popular programs. Read the reviews, talk to friends and, then try a few different application programs, either on someone else's computer, or at the store. Some retailers allow a 30-day trial period. There are many similar **application** programs, all with major to minor differences in capabilities, features, and price.

➤ Electronic Organizers

There's an inexpensive computer-like gadget which is worth considering <u>in addition to</u> a desktop PC, and even a laptop: a hand-held *Electronic Organizer*. It's the PC version of your "daytimer", and because of its pocket size, it can be carried with you *at all times*. (They are sold through electronics and office supply stores).

Casio dominates in the basic to middle portion of this market, and *Sharp* with the sophisticated models. Organizers start with credit card-sized units that simply store names and phone numbers, and go up to units about the size of an oversize wallet that have over a megabyte of memory! The latest model from Sharp is called *Zaurus* (classed as a PDA - Personal Digital Assistant), which has many of the features found on a laptop PC, plus the ability to store handwritten diagrams and notes!

Appointments, directories (including name, address, phone/cellular/fax/e-mail, birthday, etc.), memos, spreadsheets, expense records, and TO DOs, can all be carried with you. Finding a note in your written records can be slow to impossible, but with an organizer you can search *all* your records by name, date, times, area code, or place. Any of the information stored in the organizer can be printed out (provided it has a comm port), and best of all it can be "backed up" to your PC so you have a duplicate of all your vital data!

⊞🖥⌨🖱💾   *Example*   💾🖱⌨🖥⊞

Description	Store	$
💾**Software:** [1]		
⊞		
⊞*Quicken*		
⊞*TurboTax*		
⊞		
	SubTotal =	
🖥**Hardware:**		
Ultimate 586	*Computer Outlet*	
Surge protector/UPS		
Additional RAM	*Mail Order*	
Interlink Mouse		
	SubTotal =	
	System TOTAL =	

---

[1] *DOS* and *Windows* are usually bundled with a new [IBM compatible] computer. *Macs* use System 7.

My Computer System[2]

Description	Store	$
🖫Software:		
	SubTotal =	
🖳Hardware:		
	SubTotal =	
	System TOTAL =	

---

2 It's OK to photocopy this page.

➤ Laptops and Notebooks

An understanding of PCs would be incomplete without knowing about *Laptops* and *Notebooks*. Any computer that is small enough to be transported on a regular basis, is a *portable*. The fastest growing category of portables, is *Laptops*. Though they are much smaller than their *desktop* counterparts, many feature a 486 engine, with a 200-meg hard drive, and a VGA color screen.

Laptops are designed to be operated comfortably while seated in economy class on an airline; they have a full alpha-numeric keyboard but not all of the accessory keys, and a smaller (liquid crystal) screen which can display the same amount of information as a desktop VGA monitor. They run on batteries or regular (AC) power: nickel-metal-hydride and lithium-ion are more common now than ni-cad batteries. Batteries provide anywhere from 2 to 6 hours of operation depending on the model, screen type, and the intensity of your work: an extra battery is usually required on long flights. You'll pay a premium for a laptop compared to a desktop, and suffer some reduced functionality, so be sure you really need that portability.

The screen quality has improved dramatically to the point where the top models have a built-in color **VGA** screen (active matrix is the best). Running a color screen takes more

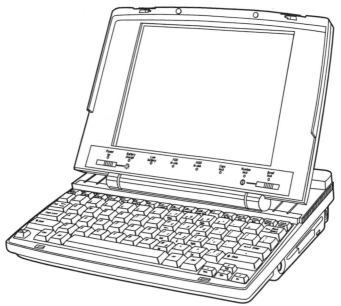

battery power: the monochrome screen is just as sharp, though less *snazzy*. Most have a built-in *mousepad* or *joystick* style mouse, which is a big improvement over the *trackball* style.

   Notebooks are a further miniaturization of the *Laptop*, and there are additional sub-categories known as *Sub-Notebooks* and *Palmtops*. Basically they achieve their compactness by using a smaller screen displaying fewer lines and by deleting the hard drive, though they do have a miniaturized full keyboard.

   Some of these portables and all pocket organizers lack a disk drive. Transferring files and downloading the portable's internal memory is slow and clumsy without the aid of a *communication link.* An innovative company, *Traveling Software*, makes a range of communication packages for portables, complete with cables: *LapLink*, *LapLink-Mac*, and *PC-Link*. Its mainstay is *Windows*-compatible *LapLink*, which is the most popular file transfer program in the world. Of course *LapLink* can also speed file transfers between two desktop PCs (over 3 MB/minute).

➠ Look for newer models that have a **PCMCIA** slot: this allows plug-in options such as flash memory, modems and LAN interfaces.

Osborne, was the first to offer the *office-on-the-go* computer in the late 70s. *Compaq* followed a few years later with a very successful series that featured an internal 10-MB hard drive. Though they heralded a new era, those portables are better known as *luggables* today.

➤ Putting your PC to work

Not everyone needs a spreadsheet or a word processor, so here are a few application programs that almost everybody can use.

Nearly every adult has a bank account, and that means the wonderful chore of reconciling once a month. Why not let the computer help? There are quite a few programs designed for the task but one outshines them all ... it's the one I use ... an inexpensive application program called

Quicken [for Windows or DOS, and Mac]. Of course it does a lot more than just your checking account: you can generate screen and paper reports with hand-holding dialog boxes that prompt you for the required parameters. Budgeting, managing loan payments and investments become a breeze! Having accurate records, and expenses that are categorized, is essential to filing a tax return with some peace of mind. Business users are better served by a program called *QuickBooks*, which has a similar easy interface along with the features business accounting needs.

If you want to be a little less dependent on a tax preparer, then consider a program named *Turbo Tax*. It's designed to automatically extract the figures for your tax return from *Quicken*. It leads you through your tax return step by step, and even alerts to you to items that might flag an audit. Virtually any printer can produce IRS approved forms, ready for filing. One version is designed for the individual or small businesses, and another full accounting package for a medium-sized business. State add-on packages are also available.

➤ What's the Internet?

It's name is a contraction of *Interconnected-Networks*: it allows computer users around the world to access an enormous wealth of electronically stored information, normally via a phone and **modem**. Spawned by the US government in 1969, it has grown rapidly, and is now the world's largest *network* linking some 10,000 smaller computer networks.

Imagine yourself back in high school and your assignment is to research the demographics of your home state. First you might check your own text books for any information, then the school's library, and perhaps you would visit the city library for the most up-to-date census data. As you scan various books, you copy the data to a notepad and begin the process of producing a report. (Elapsed time: 3hrs to 2 days). _The Internet Way:_ From the school's computer, or your home PC, you connect to the Internet and log into the US Census Bureau's database. A few clicks of the mouse later you *download* the data on your home state to your hard disk, then cut-and-paste the relevant data into your report being drafted with the PC's word processor (Elapsed time: 15 mins)!

Like a *network* of freeways that connects hundreds of cities and towns, the Internet is an invisible network using phone lines to link personal computers and mainframes around the world. Imagine planning a trip Australia: go *Downunder* on the Internet and discover the weather, geography, regions of interest, where the people live, train and airline schedules, plan around local school and public holidays, and finally download a complete satellite weather map a few days before you leave.

The term *Information Superhighway*, of which the Internet is an integral part, may be loosely defined as the ability to access, by modem and the phone line, CD-ROM, cable, or satellite, the enormous wealth of electronically stored information.

Via *Internet* you can access the latest medical research on specific subjects, send and receive messages via a personal electronic "mailbox" (*e-mail*), exchange research data, download shareware programs, files, and **driver**s from **EBB**s (BBS), see NOAA satellite weather maps, and access Library of Congress and Congressional records. With special software, a two-way (duplex) phone conversation and real time video confrencing is now possible.

Thousands of universities, companies and governments around the world have connected their enormous databases of information to the *Internet* ... all of which is accessible to you from your home or office PC, via a **modem**. Through [*Windows* application] front doors such as *Netscape, Mosaic, and WinWeb* it is possible to "roam" hundreds of subjects on the *Internet* easily (*MacWeb* is the Macintosh version*).

Can I access the Internet through commercial on-line services such as *AmericaOnline CompuServe, Delphi* and *Genie*? Yes, most on-line services now offer limited

Internet access, and for novices they are easier to use than direct access programs such as *NetScape* or *Mosaic*. The downside is they charge for on-line time and downloading of files, and may limit you to slower **modem** speeds. *AmericaOnline* (800) 827-6364, *CompuServe* (800) 554-4067, and *Delphi* (800) 695-4005.

some INTERNET lingo

Address......... Normally means your *"e-mail"* address via *AmericaOnline*, or the Internet, but it also means the *address* or location of any file, on another computer. Like your home address, you create a unique *electronic address* so that people can send you text messages or whole files, via the Internet, or your local office network. To *e-mail* a message to someone at Microsoft Corp. the address might look like this: billg@microsoft.com (Note the *address* is usually lower case, and always without spaces).

FAQ .... **F**requently **A**sked **Q**uestions [with answers] that users of the Internet or another service pose. Basically a help system for novices.

FTP .... **F**ile **T**ransfer **P**rotocol. See Protocols. A software utility for transferring programs and files over a modem.

Gopher .... Not the kind that digs holes ... more like the office *gofer* in its ability to run *electronic errands* around the Internet. It's a program that allows you to choose from menus rather than typing complicated Internet addresses.

Home page ... Normally the first screen you see when you are connected to the Internet or an on-line service (e.g. *AmericaOnline*).

Host............... A *host* computer provides services to the other computers connected via a network. Like a good party host, it attends to the requests of its guests - *a scotch on the rocks* might be a bit much.

IP................... Internet Protocol. See Protocols.

Mosiac/NetScape .... Two popular **Web** *browsers*. Allows easy *Windows* access to the Internet Web (WWW) by pointing and clicking with a mouse.

Online........... A term probably derived from "I'm **on** the [phone] **line**". In computer parlance it means your are connected to another computer, or service, via a phone/modem connection.

Packet........... Rather than sending a continuous stream of data over a phone line or radio link, data is broken into *packets*, transmitted and acknowledged before sending the next packet. This technology assures error free data transfer.

PPP .... Point-to-Point Protocol. A **protocol** that enables a computer to communicate via the Internet using **TCP/IP** over standard phone lines and high-speed **modems**.

Protocols....... In the diplomatic service *protocol* is the accumulated set of rules governing the conduct between nations. In this context *protocol* refers to the "standards governing the exchange of messages between computers". Driving *protocol* in North

America, and most of Europe, requires driving on the right side of the road ... but this *protocol* is not universal, as it doesn't work in Australia, Japan or the UK. Computers need "universal" *rules of the road* for exchanging information across town and around the world ... otherwise it would be like bumper cars at an amusement park.

SLIP .... Serial Line Internet Protocol.

TCP/IP .... Transmission Control Protocol / Internet Protocol.

Telco .... Local Telephone company.

Telnet .... A **protocol** that allows you to remotely run another computer via the **Internet**.

Web .... Short for World Wide Web, the fastest growing part of the Internet: often referred to as *the Web* in speech, and *WWW* in print. When you see an address that includes WWW, it is accessing through *the* Web e.g.: http://www.fedworld.gov/ is the US Federal Government's Information Network.

✳ NERD STUFF ✳

The *Web* is a set of hyperlinked Internet information sources that conform to a standard known as Hyper Text Markup Language. HTML in turn is a subset of the Standard Generalized Markup Language, a standard developed by the US Defense Department for cross-platform publishing.

> ### *Here's a small sample of what's on the Internet:*
> *Name* / Address / Comments

⊕ *White House* home page
http://www.whitehouse.gov/
Executive branch documents, video clips and a
voice message from the President.

⊕ *Thomas Legislative Information*
http:// thomas.loc.gov/
Library of Congress; searchable text of House and
Senate bills; and govt. leaders *e-mail* addresses.

⊕ *U.S. Bureau of Census*
http://www.census.gov/
Census news and statistical database.

⊕ *FedWorld Information Network*
http://www.fedworld.gov/
U.S. Government information with links to large
data banks such as the NTIS (Nat. Technical Info. Serv.).

⊕ *Weather*
http://www.mit.edu:8001/usa.html   *or*
http://sci-ed.fit.edu/wx.html   *or*
http://www/aviation.jsc.nasa.gov./wx.html
    Visual and infrared satellite weather maps of
USA and world regions; forecasts, regional and
local weather; and aviation info.

⊕ *Australia*
http://www.auslig.gov.au/Australi.htm   *or*
http://info.anu.edu.au/
    The *InfoSuperhighway* connection to the *Land
Downunder*. Statistical info, satellite weather maps.

⊕ *??? - Search the Web by Subject*

http://webcrawler.cs.washington.edu/WebCrawler
/WebQuery.html   *or*

http://lycos.cs/cmu.edu/

Enter a keyword, such as "Australia" or "caffeine", and this *search engine* will offer a list of **Web** sites.

➤ **Business uses for the Personal Computer**

Successful management is the control of all that is involved in operating a business, and this depends heavily on accurate information.

PCs are already widely integrated into medium and large businesses, though they are under utilized by senior management as an information manager. Of the thousands of executives using *PCs* today, most are in the high technology industries, or they manage very large companies which already operate workstations or mainframe computers. Indeed, it is estimated that only 60% of all businesses in America use a computer. The *Personal Computer* has not been adopted widely by the small businesses which most need to improve their productivity.

ANALYSIS OF COMPUTER USE BY DEPARTMENTS

💻 **MANAGEMENT:**

A strong feature of the *PC* is that it is isolated from other company computers and other forms of record keeping ... in a word ... Privacy! Its ability to perform instant *"what if"* scenarios on the company's operations makes it extremely flexible. Other advantages include a *PCs* ease of use and the large choice of inexpensive *"off-the-shelf"* application software.

The biggest impediment to executive use of *PCs* has perhaps come from the traditional typewriter keyboard which many executives associate with the clerical functions of a business. This will probably not be completely overcome until **speech recognition** systems are commonplace.

GRAPHIC PRESENTATION of DATA:

A part of management is being creative, planning for the future and seeing problems in the developmental stage. Graphics allow faster understanding of numeric information because pictures appeal to our most informative sense - *sight*. Most of us are better at remembering faces than names; it's the same with figures. Relationships between figures in a report are easier to grasp in a chart than raw figures.

🖳 ACCOUNTING:

The use of computers in accounting is widespread, and the advantages are well appreciated by management. This is normally the first area of a company's operations to be computerized.

The centralization of the accounting functions around the computer have, however, brought two problems: loss of privacy and fraud.

Loss of Privacy: With the dramatic rise in clerical wages and the arrival of smaller minicomputers in the sixties and seventies, most companies were forced to reduce their clerical staff and install a computer. A department employing ten could suddenly manage with three.

The complexity of early computer software prevented executives from operating mini computers, and so the *input* operators also became the *output* operators. The weekly and monthly financial reports containing the most sensitive information were first seen by the computer operators.

The *PC* Solution: Using *PCs* executives can communicate via a LAN with the company's main computer and work on totals and other summarized information: Access to any information can be easily controlled by passwords.

Fraud: The exchange of pencil and paper for *PCs* with magnetic storage have opened up new possibilities for the dishonest employee. The old bookkeeping system, while slow by today's standards, showed a paper trail of entries and changes, with the important feature of handwriting.

The right accounting software can overcome most of these problems by keeping a "non-erasable" trail in a separate audit file, showing the trail of entries and changes.

While the risk of fire and theft may be low, consideration should be given to keeping off-site backups to cover this possibility.

Costing: Accurate costing programs based on a spreadsheet can be easily developed in-house or by an outside consultant for a fraction of the cost it would take to write a custom program on a mainframe. Knowing the exact cost of your products is the key to knowing where your *profits and losses* are coming from.

⌨ SECRETARIAL:

The advent of computerized *"word processing"* in the 1970s resulted in a dramatic increase in output per secretary and an increased level of flexibility and creativity. Initially only affordable by the larger law firms, mailing bureaus, and government agencies, inexpensive word-processing was incorporated into the multifaceted capabilities of the *PC* in the early 1980s.

This was perhaps the first successful demonstration of the advantages of an individual computer in the office. The potential of this concept, especially in terms of electronic storage, has yet to be fully realized. Scanners (to input printed data without retyping) and laser disks (for permanent storage) will add to the utility of word-processing.

Documents can be typed, altered, proof read and checked for spelling errors by the electronic dictionary before a printed copy is produced. Errors are virtually eliminated with such features as *spell checkers*.

A spin-off of this technology is *Desktop Publishing* which allows in-house creation and publishing of newsletters, reports and graphic presentation material suitable for an overhead projector ... something which is expensive and time-consuming with an outside service.

Mailing Lists ... Computers were first used exclusively for numerical calculations; however, as more advanced software was written, huge databases could be manipulated.

Customer addresses can be recalled from memory, standard paragraphs inserted, and accounting data automatically inserted into letters to produce invoices and reminders. The advertising of products and politics, by mass mailings, came into being.

🖳 PLANT:

Inventory control is a very costly and time consuming part of any manufacturing or warehousing operation. Inexpensive PCs can track inventory by bar-code or other methods right at the factory level and transfer the results from production or shipping directly to the accounting computer.

PCs offer the possibility of factory level control of raw materials, work-in-progress and finished goods, in turn providing accurate daily information to the accounts department and management without additional data entry. Accurate daily updates, as opposed to the end of month inventory check by the accounts department, become an economic reality with inexpensive computers.

At a more sophisticated level computers can monitor a manufacturing or processing operation, and of course operate robots. Sensing devices can be used to feed information to a computer to operate automated controls and safety devices.

CAD/CAM - Automated manufacturing:

$100,000+ *Computer Aided Design* (CAD) systems have been around in larger computers for decades. However, what has revolutionized this work is the incredibly powerful software running on inexpensive microcomputers. Something that was previously only operated by GM is now available to small manufacturing businesses, opening up tremendous gains in productivity. $10,000 *PC workstation* CAD systems can now be used to design tooling in-house.

In turn this can be used by Computer Aided Manufacturing systems to run the lathes which cut the steel, resulting in a finished tooling in a fraction of the time. CAM is the most recent, most expensive, and potentially one of the most revolutionary uses of the computer. While *PCs* are being used with robotics, it is beyond the scope of this book.

➤ **PC HEALTH**

... sorry we only take patients who are in good health, have a Gold VISA, insurance, and still have their own teeth.

Maintaining your PC "in good health" is easy ... here are a few suggestions.

Power: Always "filter" the electrical power to your computer and other electronic devices with a **surge protector**, and optionally prevent data corruption caused by outages, with a **UPS**.

Screen: Turn off the monitor when it is not in use, especially overnight. A *Screen Saver* program is an automatic way, to protect it during your regular short breaks (To setup see: *Windows Program Mgr - Control Panel - Desktop*).

Anti-Static: Clean the screen with a special anti-static cleaner (*CompuKleen* 800-783-1999). Other surfaces should be wiped regularly with a moist cloth. Air cans can blast dust and dirt particles from hard to get to places.

Diskette Drive: Use a cleaning disk monthly, such as *TrackMate's "4in1"* (800) 486-5707. Dust, and especially cigarette particles, can interfere with the read/write head of your drive. (The Hard Disk Drive is hermetically sealed from dust and other pollutants).

Smoke: Never smoke near a PC. The tiny particles given off by a burning cigarette find their way into disk drive openings, and via the fan, around all the unseen internal parts.

Modifications: Never open up your PC (to add boards, etc.) without protecting the electronics from *Static Electricity*: ground yourself first.

Moving: Keep the strong cardboard boxes and molded styrofoam that your PC was packaged in ... transport or store the computer, monitor and other equipment, in those boxes only.

On/Off: There are two schools of thought about leaving your computer on continuously. *Pro*: solid state devices are thought to last longer if they are not subjected to the jolt of being turned on and off. *Con*: it's a waste of electricity, and moving parts, such as the hard drive, will wear out sooner (MTBF).

Heat: Don't keep your PC in the company greenhouse. High heat and humidity mean trouble for you computer.

➤ What's a Computer Virus?

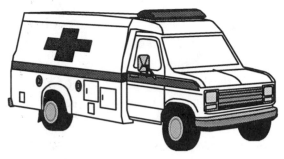

It's a misleading term to say the least ... it's not a *virus* at all. Only organic or living organisms can be affected by a virus, and a computer, no matter what anyone says, is not *alive* ... not even *Robbie the Robot* or *Hal* from *2001*.

What is it then? It's an unauthorized software program designed to completely, or partially, destroy the computer's software, often by erasing the hard disk. It is a *deliberate* attempt to cause major problems. Its closest cousin is a **Bug**, which is a programming error or oversight, which was not weeded out in the testing stage.

How does it work? After being secretly fed into the existing program code, it may lie there dormant for months until it is triggered by a certain date, password, or computer activity, such as a backup.

How does it get into the computer? Computers that are part of a network are at the greatest risk, as virtually anyone with the requisite skills can access the central computer remotely, much like a malicious *hacker*, by using a phone and a modem. On rare occasions original manufacturers' application software disks have been sabotaged, resulting in individual *PC* users loading a *virus* into their system.

What can I do to protect my computer? Don't worry! Your chances of encountering a computer *virus,* if you are not on a network, are very low. As a pain reliever you can take the *preventive* measure of installing one of the many *anti-virus* programs. Some are available at no cost from Electronic Bulletin Boards (EBB). A separate backup of all your program applications and user files is probably the best insurance against a disk erasing *virus*. Another precaution you might take is to turn the modem off when not online. Banks are so conscious of electronic security they turn their fax machines off at night.

➤ What is a Supercomputer?

These are the fastest and most expensive ($10 million+) electronic computers in existence. The military, a few universities and hi-tech research groups are the only users who can afford these *roadrunners*. In the PC world, the development cost ratio is typically 10:1 for software versus hardware; with *supercomputers* this ratio falls to 2:1. They are typically accessed with *PC* workstations via a **network**, and not operated as stand-alone computers. The US government's NOAA uses a *supercomputer* for weather predictions - processing the enormous amount of data collected from satellites, atmospheric balloons and ocean probes around the world.

Cray, the world's best known *supercomputer* series is named after its inventor, Seymour R. Cray. The other major players in this field are int_el, *Tera Computer* (Seattle WA), *Thinking Machines* (Cambridge MA), and *Kendall Square*. One parallel *supercomputer* design uses 1,000 microprocessors capable of an incredible one trillion calculations per second!

int_el's *supercomputer* is the *Touchstone Delta* which can handle 32 gigaFLOPS. By way of comparison, today's *PC*s run about .0012% of that speed. It stands 5' high, 3' deep, 16' long and is installed at *Caltech Pasadena*, California, in a room that is kept at a rather chilly temperature. It comprises 528 *i860* microprocessors (a 64-bit, 50 MHz pure racing machine), each with 16 megabytes of memory.

Tera Computer's "*roadrunner*" is designed around their own 400MHz CPU using a technique called "pipelining". Normally signals are sent down the wire and a response is received. *Pipelining* sends signals in succession without waiting for a reply, rather like a machine-gun firing a round. It's a combination of hardware design and software working within that hardware, that results in the *ultimate Supercomputer*.

Take heart, we're still better. In comparison to a *supercomputer*, the brain's performance in seeing, interpreting and *visualizing* what we see, is stunning. At the same time the brain is visualizing it is also analyzing past images for similarity, and taking in information from our ears and nose and checking that against previous experiences. Our brain's speed at processing complex, moving, color images, makes a *supercomputer* seem like a snail, even when it performs the most complex task imaginable!

Hello, my name is Buggsy ... I'm planning a graduation party!

Postscript

The electronics industry is one of the five largest industries in the world. The semiconductor part of that business grew from $1 billion to $65 billion between 1960 and 1990. By 1991 personal computer shipments exceeded the sales of mainframe and minicomputers!

For the near future, speech recognition offers the next step in the catch phrase "user friendly". Computers will take another leap when handwritten input becomes commonplace.

Ceramic materials may replace silicon, allowing communication by photon or light, which will solve some of the resistance problems encountered by electricity, allowing an ever faster processor to be built. Bio-chips with switches made from organic material such as protein, rather than transistors, are also in the works.

The greatest technological advantage the United States possesses is in software. Hardware can be reverse engineered and copied, given enough time and money, especially when such activity is being backed by government policy. Software, on the other hand, comes from creative minds - something which cannot be mimicked. This creative spirit is the explanation for the US still holding the lead in inventions, though it is not continuing the pattern established from 1850 to 1950.

Summary of the SENIOR Chapter

☐   There are two broad groupings of PCs: IBM compatibles and Apple Macintoshes.

☐   A computer has two types of <u>memory</u>: RAM, which is *temporary* and where it holds work-in-progress, and a Disk(ette) which *permanently* stores programs and user files.

☐   A <u>coprocessor</u> is a secondary microprocessor carrying part of the CPU's load.

☐   The <u>Bus</u> routes all the PC's internal communication. Its design is critical to the overall performance of a PC.

☐   System <u>performance</u> is determined by: the CPU, Clock speed, Bus and RAM speed.

☐   There are four types of desktop <u>printers</u>: Ink-jet, laser, dot-matrix, and thermal transfer.

☐   *The Internet* is a network of informational databases, which can be accessed with a PC via a phone and modem.

☐   <u>PC Health</u> care ... a few DOs and DON'Ts.

Nerd Warning: Never leave your credit card anywhere near your PC. Its close proximity may cause your PC to experience *quivering* electronic flashes at the thought of adding expensive accessories.

A Computer is a machine ... the use of which is determined by software instructions.

Can't find it in the
Terminology section?

Check the **INDEX** ...

It's a complete cross-reference catalog
of all the **Bold face terms** and other
selected terms used in the book.

Some of the terms listed in this section are discussed in greater detail in the tutorial chapters, from Freshman *to* Senior.

◆

1.4 MB ..... 🖫   1.44 **m**ega**b**ytes or 1,440,000 bytes of data. This is the (high density) capacity of a rigid 3½" magnetic **diskette**. A *Mac* 3½" (high density) diskette stores 1.2 MB. See Byte, 720KB.

386................. See 80386.

486 .... See 80486 for int**e**l's version. *Cyrix* and *AMD* offers an excellent line of competively priced 486 microprocessors. *Cyrix* also offers a *486* plug-compatible upgrade for a *386* computer.

586 .... See *Pentium* for int**e**l's version. *Cyrix* and *NexGen* have developed competing designs known as the *K5* and *Nx586* which are compatible running *DOS, Windows and OS/2* operating systems.

686................. int**e**l's successor to the 150MHz *Pentium* which has been identified as P6 during development. The first version (133MHz) is scheduled for release in late '95.

6800............... *Motorola* family of 8-bit microprocessors which were used in the *Apple* line of personal computers. Succeeded by the **68000**.

68000............. *Motorola* family of 16-bit / 8 MHz microprocessors which are used in the *Apple Macintosh* line of personal computers. It derives its name from the number of transistors that make up the processor: 68,000. The last two digits are the model number within the series: odd numbers are used for enhancements and even for new versions.

68010............. An enhanced *Motorola* 68000 microprocessor.

68020............. A new version of the *Motorola* 68000 microprocessor running at 16 MHz.

68030............. An enhanced *Motorola* 68020 microprocessor running at 16, 20, 25 or 40 MHz.

68040............. A new version of the *Motorola* 68020 microprocessor. There is no enhanced version (68050); however, a new version called the 68060 is planned for the future.

720 KB.......... ⊟ 720 kilobytes or 720,000 bytes of data. Normally used to measure the capacity of a (double density) 3½" magnetic disk. A Mac (double density) diskette stores 800KB. See Byte.

8086............... In 1978 intel introduced its first 16-bit **microprocessor** known as the *80-86*. The *clock speed* ran at 5, 8, or 10 MHz.

8088............... A slower 8-bit **bus** version of the intel *8086* microprocessor was selected by *IBM* for its first *PC* in 1981. It has a *clock speed* of 5 or 8 MHz, very slow by today's standard. All IBM, *Compaq* and compatible (clone) computers use an intel microprocessor.

80286............. In 1982 intel introduced an improved 16-bit **microprocessor** known as the *80286*, which included such advanced features as **multitasking** and **virtual** memory management. It comprises 130,000 transistors with an average speed of 1 **MIPS**. The *clock speed* ran 8, 10 or 12.5 MHz which meant about 50% improvement in performance. This is the CPU used in the *IBM AT* and *Compaq 286*.

80287............. The intel **coprocessor** developed for the *80286*.

80386............. In 1985 intel introduced a 32-bit **microprocessor** known as the *80386*, which included paged memory support for modern operating systems. Advanced new features and compatibility with older software written for the earlier processors has been a hallmark of intel's microprocessor development. In 1988 a cost-reduced 16-bit *80386SX* was introduced that could handle all the new 32-bit software. It comprises 500,000 transistors and performance has been continuously improved by offering higher clock speeds resulting in a boost in processing from 6 to 12 million instructions per second (mips). There are three versions of the *386*: *80386SX* 16-bit bus; clock speed 16-20 MHz. *80386DX* 32-bit bus; clock speed 16-33 MHz. *80386SL* laptop version-16-bit bus; 20-25 MHz.

80387............. The int**e**l math **coprocessor** developed for the *80386*.

80486............. Introduced in 1989, this is the current *state-of-the-art* **microprocessor** from int**e**l with a 32-bit **bus**, a **clock speed** from 25 to 66MHz and, in the case of the *DX,* a built-in math **coprocessor**. It contains 1.2 million **transistors**, delivers twice the performance (20 Million Instructions Per Second) compared to the *386*, and is 100% compatible with software written for the *386*. There are two versions of the 32-bit *486*:

80486SX   - 80 MB bus band width   and a clock speed of   16-25   Mhz.
80486SX2   -   a   clock   speed   of   50   Mhz
80486DX   -   160   MB   bus   band   width   and a clock speed of 25-50 MHz.
80486DX2   - on a 25mhz motherboard this runs at 50mhz and on a 33mhz it runs at   66MHz).
80486DX4   -   a tripled CPU - either 75 Mhz or 100 MHz.

80586............. See *586* and *Pentium*.

AI .... See **A**rtificial **I**ntelligence.

Alert Box .... A term for a box which appears on
 the screen with warnings
requiring your response. In
all *Windows* and *Mac*
application programs, for
example, an *alert box* appears when you try to exit,
asking you if you want to *save* your work first.

AMD .... **A**dvanced **M**icro **D**evices - a US
manufacturer of int**e**l compatible microprocessors.
It has adopted int**e**l's model numbers and is
identified by the abbreviation *Am*, (e.g.
Am486DX2-80, *Pentium* equivalent is K5, an
abbreviation of **K**ryptonite**5**86).

Apple .... Computer company founded by
Steven Jobs and Steven Wozniak in 1976. The
Apple II, introduced in 1977, was one of the earliest
successful personal computers employing the newly
developed technology of the **microprocessor**. It
was the first PC to adopt the Xerox developed
Graphical User Interface (icons) and mouse. It was
followed by the *Apple IIR*, *IIe, IIc* and the less
successful *Apple III*. See also Mac.

Artificial Intelligence .... A branch of computer
science that is trying to simulate the human thought
process. Also known as "*AI*". Computers follow a
prewritten set of instructions (software) and have no
possibility of learning by trial and error, such as any
child routinely does for himself. An example would
be to program a computer about light and electricity
and then propose a question such as *"Why is the*

light bulb not on?", causing the computer to develop combinations of possibilities that it was not preprogrammed with. A child, by comparison, who knows nothing of physics, would probably look at the wall switch and point out it has not been turned on. We call this *common sense*, and it is such natural attributes which baffle the efforts of scientists to achieve anything like our intelligence. How would a computer, which after all is a machine, handle *feelings* and *emotions*?

Assembler Code ...... A language processor that translates symbolic assembly language into equivalent Machine Code or machine language (1s & 0s), which is required by the computer hardware.

ASCII .... Pronounced *as-kee*, it is an acronym for **A**merican **S**tandard **C**ode for **I**nformation **I**nterchange. A standardized table for representing letters from the alphabet and numbers, as 8-digit **binary numbers** (machine code). ASCII is used microcomputers, terminals and printers allowing communication between differing makes and models. For us it would be equivalent to a universal alphabet allowing easier communication between all the nations of the world. Saving a file as ASCII code strips its format codes but allows it to be read by almost every computer program.

ATM .... Acronym for **A**dobe **T**ype **M**anager, an inexpensive program for *Windows* or *Mac* PCs which greatly improves the sharpness of both screen and printed characters. It works with *Postscript* and non-*Postscript* printers. Also **A**synchronous

Transfer Mode, a high speed digital communication system for computers.

Autoexec.Bat.......Abbreviation for *Auto-exec*uting *Bat*ch file. This is the second file, after *Config.Sys*, *MS-DOS* looks for in the root directory when the computer is turned on. This batch file, which can be modified by the user, defines the characteristics of each device connected to your system.

Backup ....An operation which duplicates software programs for security. See **Backups are Vital!**

Bar code ....||ıııııı||ıı|ı| A series of short, vertical, tall and short, or **thick** and thin lines (**binary**), which can be read by an optical scanning device. The Bar Code represents a *unique digital* number which has been assigned to the item. Various bar code standards are in use, including:

2 of 5   Shipping Container format.
4-5-1   Recording Industry format.
Code 39   Inventory Management format.
EAN   European Article Number - publish'g.
ISBN   EAN 978 publishing format (back cover).
UPC   Universal Price Code - retail market.
      Other formats include: Code 128, Logmar and Coda bar. The most common is the UPC code found on nearly every item sold at supermarkets. This code can be scanned by a laser beam enabling computerized inventory control and accurate pricing at the checkout.

BASIC ....Acronym for *Beginner's All-purpose Symbolic Instruction Code.* One of the easiest and most popular computer languages (developed by

John Kemeny and Thomas Kurtz, 1965-70). Its great advantage is the use of English language commands such as IF, GOTO, +, -, *, /, and PRINT. Most versions of *MS-DOS* come with *BASIC*.

Baud .... Usually expressed as *"Baud rate"*. A unit that measures the speed of data transmission, by the number of electrical oscillations that occur each second. Also expressed in (bps) *bits per second*, though they are not necessarily equivalent. Originally it was equivalent to twice the number of Morse Code dots transmitted continuously per second. Modems communicating via a telephone line typically transfer data back and forth between 1200 and 9600 Baud. Printers typically receive data over a special printer cable and are therefore able to communicate at a much faster rate of 19200 Baud, whereas a modem is limited by the phone line and must use a lower speed of 2400, 9600 or now 28,800. See also bps. [Named after the French inventor of a telegraph code, *Baudot* 1845-1903].

BBS .... **B**ulletin **B**oard **S**ervice better known as an **Electronic Bulletin Board**.

Billion .... A cardinal number equaling one thousand million: (a trillion is one thousand billion).
American/French. $1,000,000,000 = 1 \times 10^9$
British.................. $1,000,000,000,000 = 1 \times 10^{12}$

Binary .... A generic word meaning TWO. As with the dots and dashes of *Morse code*, computers use a primitive **binary** language consisting of 0 and 1, the result of a computer "switch" being OFF or ON. Binary numbers are Base-2 (0-1) as opposed to the decimal system we are familiar with which is Base-10 (0-9). The decimal number 58 appears as "**111010**" in binary notation ($1x2^5 + 1x2^4 + 1x2^3 + 0x2^2 + 1x2^1 + 0x2^0$). Binary numbers contain more digits than their decimal equivalent, making them cumbersome for people to use. This was largely overcome by the development of advanced programming languages which use English word instructions and which can be **compiled** back into **machine code** (binary digits) for the computer to read.

Decimal	Binary
$2^0 = 1$	1
$2^1 = 2$	10
3	11
$2^2 = 4$	100
5	101
$2^3 = 8$	1000
$2^4 = 16$	10000

Letters (A-Z, a-z) and other characters we routinely use (e.g.: $, @, &, !, ., {}) are assigned a binary code which is stored in a computerized table for the computer to have instant access.

BIOS .... Acronym for **B**asic **I**nput/**O**utput for the **S**ystem. **DOS** depends on the BIOS to handle low-level routines, such as putting characters on the screen, reading keystrokes, and read/write disk functions. Such operations are so frequent they are stored in a BIOS **ROM** *chip,* located on the **motherboard**, rather than in DOS software.

Bit .... A contraction of the words: *binary digit*. The smallest unit of data used by a computer which is either a "0" or a "1". Each character that we use (a, A, 8) is made up of 8 *bits*, actually 8 zeros and ones which is one *byte* of machine code or computer language. Eight bits make up a byte. See also binary, bps, and byte.

Board............ Expansion *boards* are so named because they comprise electronic circuits and *chips* on a thin 12"x4" *board*. These are fitted into expansion *slots* either on the *motherboard* or an expansion chassis. Expansion boards are generally used for extra RAMemory, upgrading the video system and for **peripheral** devices such as scanners.

Boot................ Usually expressed as - *Boot-Up*, meaning to start a computer and load the software into memory; *Reboot*, start the computer again; *Warm-reboot*, reload the application program again in the middle of a session; *Cold-boot*, restart the computer by turning the power switch off and on and reload everything. The *Boot* sector of a **disk** is the very first to be read at startup.

bps.................. Acronym for **b**its **p**er **s**econd. A measurement of the speed of data transfer between two computer devices such as a printer, **network** or a **modem**. Utilizing special cable rates up to 500,000 bps are possible. See Baud, bit, CCITT & Modem.

Buffer............. A device for temporarily storing data that is being transferred between devices with differing transmission/receive speeds. This may be internal to the computer such as a disk or RAM *buffer*, or it may be external peripheral device such as a print *buffer*. Typically, a computer sends data to a printer at a rate faster than the printer can handle, which necessitates a *buffer*.

Bug............... Any error in a computer program (software). Its origin came from a technician who found the offending problem in an early vacuum tube relay computer. Using tweezers he removed an insect that was stuck between the contact points of a relay switch ... and triumphantly exclaimed: "*I found the bug!*"

Bus............... It's the main pathway of communication in a computer. Refer to **What Does the BUS do?** for a detailed explanation.

Button............ A term used in the *Windows/Mac* environment for a box button image on screen. *Clicking* on the *button* with a mouse simulates pushing a button with one's finger.

Byte............... A byte is the smallest meaningful piece of data since it represents one normal character we use (e.g.: R u 4 PCs ?). This one alphanumeric character represented by a byte, is made up of eight *bits*, which are represented by 0s and 1s. Bytes, usually expressed as kilobytes (**KB**) and megabytes (**MB**), are used to measure the capacity of a computer's memory. Example: 640 kilobytes or 2 megabytes of **RAM**, and 40 megabytes of **disk** capacity.

Cache...................... Pronounced *cash*. Its purpose is to reduce the time it takes the computer to access data. A *cache* is created by setting aside a portion of the computer's memory (**RAM**) to hold a duplicate of the data which is frequently accessed by the **CPU.** Two common types of caches are *memory* and *disk caches*. Both types store the data in RAM so it is only in existence while the computer is on. Retrieving data from RAM (transistors) is much faster than retrieving it from a [mechanical] disk. The intₑl *80486* processor has a built-in 8K memory cache. It's is like having a duplicate set of all the papers you are going to need today in a folder on your desk, rather than retrieving each one from the filing cabinet as it is needed.

CAD/CAM .... **C**omputer **A**ided **D**esign / **C**omputer **A**ided **M**anufacturing. (See CIM)

Carpal Tunnel Syndrome ... A common disorder of the wrist or hand characterized by pain, tingling, or muscular weakness. It is caused by pressure on the median nerve in the wrist and can be triggered by keyboard operations, trauma, rheumatoid arthritis, or edema of pregnancy. Short term supplementation with Vitamin B_6 may help - consult your doctor.

CCITT .... Acronym for **C**onsulting **C**ommittee for **I**nternational **T**elephone and **T**elegraph. The group which sets international communication standards for modems, networks and FAX machines. See Baud, bps, & Modem.

CD-ROM ..... Acronym for **C**ompact **D**isk-**R**ead **O**nly **M**emory. A 5" sealed plastic disk used to store data digitally (0 & 1), with a typical capacity of 680 MB, which is sufficient to store the text of a 20-volume encyclopedia. A laser beam is used to read the disk's surface which comprises a series of *pits* and *lands* of various lengths. The technology is more reliable, though slower, as it is optical (laser) rather than magnetic.

CGA.............. Acronym for **C**olor **G**raphics **A**dapter. IBM's first generation graphics standard for the *PC* monitor introduced in 1981. Offered 4 colors and 320x200 pixel resolution. See EGA, VGA, & SVGA.

Chip .... Popular name for an Integrated Circuit (**IC**), but actually a *chip* is just the semiconducting material upon which all the miniature transistors and circuits are placed. Generally square in shape, and only a ¼-inch square, it is cut from a larger wafer of the same material, usually silicon. See also *IC*, intel, & Transistor.

CIM .... Acronym for **C**omputer **I**ntegrated **M**anufacture. See CAD.

Clipboard .... A temporary *holding* area in the computer's RAM. It allows text and/or graphics to be *cut* or *copied*, and then pasted into any other file, application, or any part of the existing file.

Clock speed ...... Normally measured in **MHz**, or millions of cycles [per second], it is one of the four factors which determines the overall speed of a computer. A steady increase in the **CPU**'s *clock speed* from 8, 12, 16, 20, 25, 33, 50 and now 66

MHz has meant spectacular improvements in loading time, screen redraws, and all operations of the computer. Each clock cycle represents one instruction being processed by the computer's Central Processing Unit (CPU). Thus, a 33MHz computer can process, at least in theory, 33 million instructions per second, or *mips*. Most computers also have a separate *real-time* clock chip to keep track of the time (powered by a lithium battery). ➲ *Clock-doubler* & *OverDrive*.

Clone.............. ☺☺ Any non-*IBM* personal computer which is designed to run *Microsoft DOS*-based software on an int_el 8086, 8088, 80286, 80386, 80486 microprocessor. Normally referred to as a *PC* which is 100% *IBM* compatible. IBM designed its *PC* using freely available parts and in other cases made it a policy to have *"open architecture"* which makes it possible for other manufacturers to build *look-alikes* without violating any patents. The int_el microprocessor is patented, so nearly all PCs have the same *engine*.

Cluster.......... The smallest chunk of **data** that the *disk* controller is able to read from or write to is a *sector* of 512 **bytes**. Because there are so many sectors on a **disk** (a 1.2 MB disk has 1.2/.000512=2344 sectors) *DOS* keeps track of contiguous sectors, called *clusters*. *Clusters* are therefore the building blocks of *disk* storage.

COMDEX .... The world's largest computer convention held twice each year (Fall & Spring) in the US to display the latest developments in hardware and software. The Fall convention, which draws over 200,000 visitors, is held at the Las Vegas Convention Center in November. The smaller Spring show is held in Chicago. Although a large representation of international visitors and exhibitors attend the US COMDEX shows, there are a number of COMDEX conventions outside the US. COMDEX is an acronym for COMputer Dealers EXchange.

CompuServe .... An on-line information service users subscribe to, for business and consumer services. Connection is normally via a **modem** and a phone. See Internet.

Config.Sys .... Abbreviation for *Config*uration *Sys*tem file. After starting your computer this is the first file *MS-DOS* looks for in the root directory. It specifies which devices to install (e.g.: *mouse*) and which device drivers to use.

Conventional Memory....... This is the basic type of memory found on all computers. In a DOS-based computer it is the first 640KB of the Random Access Memory (**RAM**). Anything over 640KB is called *Extended Memory*.

Coprocessor .... Another processor which works in conjunction with the central processor (CPU). See "What is a Coprocessor" on page 105.

Copy protection .... 🖫🖫 Software is like the creative work in a book and as such is protected by copyright laws. In an effort to thwart unauthorized copies being made, special features are included on the original disk versions which either prevents the Operating System (DOS) from copying the disk or allows just one backup copy to be made.

CP/M .... Acronym for **C**ontrol **P**rogram for **M**icrocomputers. An operating system widely used on the first 16-64K microcomputers. The most common operating system today is *MS-DOS*.

 **CPU** .... Acronym for **C**entral **P**rocessing **U**nit where the software (instructions) are processed or *acted upon*. The computer's *brain*, which moves data from one RAM memory location to another, performs basic math calculations and follows (logic) branches in the programming instructions. Generally used to mean the *chip* which comprises all the essential circuitry of a computer, but a more correct definition is that it contains only the Control Unit which directs the system operations and the arithmetic/logic unit. Its processing power is determined by the number of transistors that are packed onto the *chip*, how many *bits* it processes in each clock cycle (16, 32 or 64), and its clock speed or how many cycles it makes in a second (33, 66 or 150 MHz). On each cycle it *gulps* an instruction or computes a result, and it is doing this from up to 150 million times a second! The CPU, also referred to as a the central processor and in a *microcomputer*, a *microprocessor*, is an integrated circuit (IC) on a single *chip* made of silicon. See also Microprocessor, Coprocessor, AmD, Cyrix, intel, Motorola, & *OverDrive*.

Crash............. 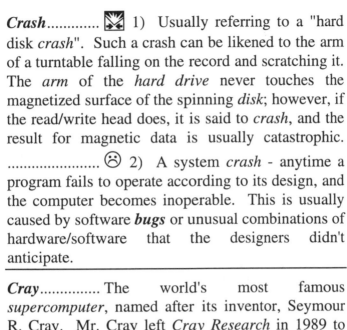 1) Usually referring to a "hard disk *crash*". Such a crash can be likened to the arm of a turntable falling on the record and scratching it. The *arm* of the *hard drive* never touches the magnetized surface of the spinning *disk*; however, if the read/write head does, it is said to *crash*, and the result for magnetic data is usually catastrophic.

.... ☹ 2) A system *crash* - anytime a program fails to operate according to its design, and the computer becomes inoperable. This is usually caused by software *bugs* or unusual combinations of hardware/software that the designers didn't anticipate.

Cray............... The world's most famous *supercomputer*, named after its inventor, Seymour R. Cray. Mr. Cray left *Cray Research* in 1989 to form a new company *Cray Computer Corp*.

CRT .... Acronym for **C**athode **R**ay **T**ube - the screen or monitor where the computer displays its messages to us. A TV screen is also a CRT, and it's also a Vacuum Tube.

Cyrix............. A US manufacturer of **int**e**l** compatible microprocessors. It has adopted int**e**l's model numbers and is identified by the abbreviation *Cx*, (e.g. Cx486SLC/25).

Data .... Individual facts, statistics, or items of information. Its singular form is Datum. [Latin *"something given"*]

Database....... 🖳 An organized body of data (information) on any subject, able to be manipulated by a computer program. A telephone directory is a (non-electronic) hierarchical database, containing names, addresses and phone numbers. See **What's a Database?** in the **Sophomore** chapter.

DD.................. Acronym for **D**ouble **D**ensity. This refers to the storage capacity of a **diskette**, typically 360 kilobytes for the 5¼" or 720 kB for the 3½". Either a *Double* or *High Density* disk drive can safely **format** a *DD* disk. (See also Diskette, HD)

DDE............... Acronym for **D**ynamic **D**ata **E**xchange: Easy transfer of data between *Windows* applications.

DDL............... Acronym for **D**ynamic **D**ata **L**ink: Easy linking of data between *Windows* applications.

Desktop......... Computer - A system consisting of a computer box, monitor, and keyboard, the size of which requires a desktop for normal use. With a Tower, or Mini-tower design the computer box sits on the floor to save desk space. The term is also used in *Desktop Publishing*. (See Laptop)

Device............ A peripheral piece of equipment that is, or can be, connected to a computer.

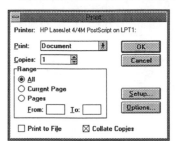

Dialog Box ....A term for a box or small window which appears on the screen with questions requesting your response. In all *Windows* and *Mac* application programs, for example, a *dialog box* appears when you select the print command, asking you how many copies you want and offering other options. Compare *Alert Box*.

Diskette......... 🖫 It's a removable/portable storage device which is used to permanently store computer data. The *diskette*, which is enclosed inside a protective square jacket, is actually a circular piece of mylar film with magnetic particles on the disk surface which records the computer's digital code, much like music recording tape. Data can be erased by reformatting, by *writing* new data over the old, or the disk being near a magnet. The early 8" and original *IBM PC* 5¼" are known as *floppy disks*. Its storage capacity (kB, MB) is determined by the *tracks per inch*, or TPI. In the case of the 5¼" disk, successive improvements have gone from 180kB to 360kB to 1.2MB, before being phased out in favor of the smaller 3½" diskette, which now outsells the 5¼" by 3:1. *Apples* were the first to use the rigid-case 3½" diskette which comes in two capacities: high and low density. The *high* density normally stores 1.4 MB of data magnetically and the *low* 720 KB. Optical 3½" diskettes are non-magnetic but look the same. Two to 4MB capacity diskettes are available for a premium, but they usually require a new disk drive. ➲ *Floppy Disk*, DD, HD, Hard Disk.

Size	DISK	Density	Capacity	PC
5¼"		DD	360 Kb	IBM
5¼"		HD	1.2 Mb	IBM
3½"		DD	720 Kb	IBM
3½"		HD	1.44 Mb	IBM
3½"		DD	800 Kb	Mac
3½"		HD	1.4 Mb	Mac

DOS .... Acronym for **D**isk **O**perating **S**ystem. It's the basic software program that enables a computer to operate: the interface between the keyboard, screen, central processing unit (CPU), and the disk drives. In general usage *DOS* has come to mean *MS-DOS* or *PC-DOS,* but it is a generic term applying to all Operating Systems that are disk-based. *MS* is an abbreviation for the developer, Microsoft Corp., and *PC-DOS* is the name used by IBM. *Apple* uses a different operating system called *Apple DOS*, and the latest operating system for the *Mac* is called *System 7.5.*

DRAM .... Pronounced *D-RAM*: Acronym for **D**ynamic **RAM** (Random Access Memory). Invented by intel it is the most common type of memory chip in personal computers. Compared to SRAMs they are inexpensive but inherently slow and need to be rewritten to regularly to preserve their memories (capacitor must be kept charged). They come in 256KB, 1, 4 and 16MB configurations. (See RAM, SIMMS)

Driver .... A mini program, resident in RAM (**TSR**), which is required for each computer device such as a printer or a **mouse**. Drivers are required for each device that is added to the basic computer system as each device from each manufacturer is a little different and the computer must be able to communicate correctly with each one.

DS .... Acronym for **D**ouble **S**ided, usually referring to a *Double Sided* Diskette. This means data can be written to both sides of the diskette. (See also Diskette, HD)

DSP .... Acronym for **D**igital **S**ignal **P**rocessor. A feature on newer **sound card**s which takes the load off the CPU: used by **speech recognition,** multimedia special effects, and compress/decompression of audio and video files.

Dumb Terminals .... Screen and keyboard connected to a multi-user computer via a cable or a modem. Incapable of functioning as a computer on its own.

EDP............... Acronym for **E**lectronic **D**ata **P**rocessing. Often referred to as the *DP Dept*.

EGA.............. Acronym for **E**nhanced **G**raphics **A**dapter. IBM's second generation graphics standard for the *PC* monitor introduced in 1984. Offered 16 colors and 640x350 pixel resolution.

EISA .... Pronounced *E-Sa*. Acronym for **E**xtended **I**ndustry **S**tandard **A**rchitecture - a 16/32-bit **bus** system introduced in 1988. It was developed by nine IBM competitors, led by *Compaq Computer Corp.*, in response to *IBM's* **Micro Channel Architecture** (MCA). EISA offers backward compatibility with the earlier **ISA** bus, whereas MCA does not. The *Mac's* bus is called *NuBus*.

EBB............... Acronym for **E**lectronic **B**ulletin **B**oard. A service available to anyone with a computer and a **modem**, usually for a small monthly fee. The term originates from the old "bulletin board" found in offices, high schools, Post Offices, and supermarkets. *AmericaOnline* and *CompuServe* are commercial services where users can exchange messages, known as **E-Mail**, or access information databases, such as news, travel, shopping and finances. Many user groups, libraries, and universities run free *EBB*s to help users solve problems, and exchange information. See Internet.

E-Mail........... ⊟ vs. ⊟⇔⊟ Abbreviation for **E**lectronic-**Mail**, normally via a PC network or **Internet**. *E-Mailing* is communicating with text messages between computers, via a **server**, which allocates disk space as "mailboxes". Privacy is maintained with message retrieval via a password.

Extended Memory............... In a DOS-based computer the first 640KB of Random Access Memory (**RAM**) is called *Conventional Memory*. Memory beyond 1 MB is called *Extended Memory*.

Extended memory requires a special driver and a *80286* processor or better. A computer sold today is typically configured with 2 megabytes (MB) of **RAM,** meaning it has 640 KB of *conventional* and 1,384 KB of *extended* memory. (See DOS, Upper Memory).

FAT............... Acronym for **F**ile **A**llocation **T**able. A magnetic disk uses a *table* to maintain the status of all the contiguous *sectors*. Contiguous *sectors* (2 to 8) are known as *clusters*.

Field.............. In a database a *field* is the smallest piece of information such as a person's last name, first name, salary, start date, or address. A group of associated *fields* is called one **record** and one or more associated *records* makes a database **file**.

File................ Computers can store massive amounts of data but without a filing system it is useless. Data which is contiguous, such as text in a letter or a spreadsheet, is named and stored as a single computer *file*. See *Root Directory* for a diagram.

File extension .... Filenames are often followed by a period, as a separator, and an *extension* to identify types of files. Each **application** program uses its own (usually unique extension) such as, *.WKS (Lotus Worksheet), *.XLS (Excel Worksheet), *.XLC (Excel Chart). The following are the most common file extensions:

*.BAK   **Back**up (duplicate file)
*.BAT   **Bat**ch (mini user program)
*.DOC   **Doc**ument (word processing file)

*.COM	**Com**mand (DOS file)
*.EXE	**Exe**cute (Application program)
*.SYS	**Sys**tem (DOS file).

File format ... .Computerized data such as a business letter usually has hidden· format{XE "Format"}· codes (word spacing & paragraph marks, etc)· attached· to· the· text.¶ Such codes tell the computer, and printer, how to display the letter: for example paragraph endings, point size, font style, and margins are all typically part of a computer **file**. By defining various standard file formats, different application programs, and even *PC* to *Mac* exchanges, can be achieved while retaining the formatting. The following are the most common standard file formats:

DCA - Document Content Architecture.

DOS Text - Unformatted text (ASCII).

RTF (*.rtf) - Rich Text Format, saves all formatting.

Text (*.txt) - Unformatted text (ASCII)

Graphics file format:

EPS - Encapsulated PostScript.

PICT - Mac and DOS compatible.

TIFF - Tagged Image File Format.

File Server .... A central data-storage device which is part of a local area **network** (LAN), or an **E-Mail**/information network such as **Internet**. Such a system is sophisticated as it must handle simultaneous requests from different users, keep track of changes, and above all, be fast. A network simply allows different users to exchange data without swapping disks, whereas a *server* allows many users to have access to a centrally updated file. A disk server by comparison is simply a remote disk drive on a LAN where the users manage the access to and updating of files.

Flash memory .... Similar to Random Access Memory (RAM) *chips* which can be erased and rewritten to rapidly, but unlike RAM *chips* these memory *chips* do not lose the stored data when the power is turned off. It is a more expensive option than magnetic disk storage, but in laptops where low power consumption, space, and weight are critical, they are catching on. ➲ **PCMCIA**

Floppy Disk .... 🖫 Any of a number of non-rigid disks used to permanently store computer data magnetically. Early designs used in *mini* computers were 8-inch, but by 1976 this was reduced to 5¼". In 1981 *IBM* adopted the 5¼" disk for its *PC* which stored 360 KB. This has been improved successively to 720 KB and now 1.2 MB. Sales of the 5¼" *floppy* peaked in 1988, and it is rapidly being replaced by the *Apple* designed rigid-case 3½-inch **diskette**. (See Diskette, Hard Disk)

FLOPS .... Acronym for **F**loating **P**oint **O**perations **p**er **S**econd. FLOPS are basically additions, subtractions, multiplications, and divisions and like **MIPS**, it is one of the methods of measuring of the speed of a computer. Expressed as KFLOPS (KiloFLOPS-thousands), MFLOPS (MegaFLOPS-millions), GFLOPS (GigaFLOPS-billions) and TFLOPS (TeraFLOPS-trillions).

Font............... A set of characters with a unique design (typeface), size (points), pitch (spacing) and style (bold, italic). The following are examples of some popular *fonts*, some of which are used in this book:

Courier (13 pts), Helvetica (9 pts), Helvetica (11 pts), *H e l v e t i c a* (13 pts, wide spacing & italic). See Typeface.

Format...................... Before the specially coated surface of a magnetic disk can be *written to*, or *read from*, it must be *formatted* by the operating system, such as MS-**DOS**, *System 7* or *UNIX*. On a *Mac* it is also known as *Initializing*.

FORTRAN .... **For**mula **Tran**slation - High level programming language mainly used in science, engineering and by the Department of Defense.

FTP............... **F**ile **T**ransfer **P**rotocol used to transfer text and files in binary form via the **Internet**.

Gigabyte....... One billion (10^9) or one thousand million bytes [of data]. Compare kilo & mega. [From Greek *gigas*, giant]

GUI............... Acronym for **G**raphical **U**ser **I**nterface, pronounced *gooey*. *Images* or *icons* replace words on the screen to initiate commands. First used by *Apple* for its game computers, it is now used widely in such environments as *Windows*.

Hacker .... 💣 A nickname for a persistant person who *hacks* at his computer until he solves the problem. A Hacker who accesses computers in an unauthorized manner, often for fun or to steal secrets, is known as a *cracker* because he *cracks* codes. Crackers usually operate via phone modems, in some cases from another country. The connectivity afforded by computer networks such as *MilNet* (Military Network) make it extremely difficult to stop skilled *cackers* once they get access to a low-level computer on a classified network.

Hard copy ..... 🖺 Normally a computer printout, as opposed to a screen report. See Hardware.

Hard Disk..... 🖴 A permanent magnetic storage device, normally built-in, which can also be an external or peripheral device. One of the main Input/Output devices of a computer. Storage capacity is measured in megabytes (MB). Also called a *Hard Drive* which is actually the whole unit, the *hard disk* being just the disk inside.

HD................. Acronym for **H**igh **D**ensity. This refers to the storage capacity of a **diskette**, typically 1.2 megabytes for the 5¼" or 1.44 MB for the 3½". Only a *High Density* disk drive can safely **format** a HD disk. (See Diskette, DS)

HIMEM........ Pronounced *HI-MEM*: Abbreviation for the **Hi**gh **Mem**ory Area (HMA) of a DOS-based computer's memory (RAM). The HMA is the first 64 KB of ***Extended Memory***, that is above 640 KB of ***Conventional Memory***. To make more *conventional memory* available to application programs, *DOS 5.0* can be loaded into the HMA along with device drivers.

Hot key .... *Pop Up* applications (**TSR**s) such as a screen calculator or appointment calendar remain in RAM until activated by special keystrokes known as a *Hot key*. Usually defined by the user it could be a combination keystroke such as *"Ctrl (Control) H"*.

Hypertext ..... Various "objects", such as text, pictures, music, or a program, are *linked* to each other. The "little hand" which appears in the *Windows* Help screen provides a good example of the fast access, by double-clicking, to various subjects spread throughout the Help database. Invented by Ted Nelson in the 1960s.

I/O .... **I**nput/**O**utput. Peripheral devices which are connected to a computer, such as the screen, keyboard and mouse, by which data is *entered into* or *received from* the computer, are called I/O devices.

IBM .... The registered name and trademark of **I**nternational **B**usiness **M**achines (*aka "I've Been Moved, International Big Mother, Itty Bitty Machines, It's Better Manually*). The world's largest and undoubtedly best known computer company. Though the company predates the computer era and did not invent the first computers, it is best known as the *computer giant* due to its incredibly successful marketing efforts masterminded by Tom Watson, Jr. IBM saw the increasingly powerful

Personal Computer as a threat to its existing line, rather than the way of the future. See OS/2.

IC .... Acronym for **I**ntegrated **C**ircuit - A semi-conducting wafer of silicon, upon which miniaturized transistors, resistors, and capacitors are *integrated* to form a *circuit*. In 1952 a British scientist named Drummer proposed the idea of an IC but was unable to make it work. Kilby, who worked for Texas Instruments (*TI*), perfected the idea in 1959 by placing miniature transistors, capacitors (charge holding component), and resistors on a tiny wafer of germanium. In 1962 the *IC* went into mass production at Fairchild and *TI*, and it was at this time they were nicknamed *Chips*. The challenge became placing more circuits on a *chip*, rather than shrinking the already tiny *IC*, something which is still going on today. The *IC* made the next and current development possible, namely *a computer on a chip* - see intel. *IC*s are divided into five classes based on the number of electronic components per *chip*:

SSI__ Small Scale Integration: < 100.
MSI _ Medium Scale Integration: 100-3,000.
LSI__ Large Scale Integration: 3,000-100,000.
VLSI __ Very Large Scale Integration: 100,000-1,000,000.
ULSI __ Ultra Large Scale Integration: >1,000,000.

IDE .... Acronym for **I**ntegrated **D**rive **E**lectronics. The standard, low-cost, hard disk drive interface for IBM compatibles, supporting transfer rates of 7.5 megabits /second. **E-IDE** (Enhanced-

IDE) is an improved standard in response to **SCSI**, which is a competing interface.

InstantOn...... A new technology to save power: the PC powers down into a *sleep state*, but instantly returns to *life* by any mouse/keyboard action.

int**e**l .... The world's largest *chipmaker*, int**e**l is an international manufacturer of microcomputer components, modules and systems. int**e**l developed **DRAM** and the first **microprocessor** (4004) in 1971. Its line of PC microprocessors includes the *8086*, *80286*, *80386, 80486*, **Pentium** *(586)* and the **P6** (686), one of which is the basic component of most *IBM* compatible PCs. Its '91 market share for 32-bit microprocessors was 66%, compared to *Motorola's* 13%. Its name is an abbreviated form of **INT**egrated **EL**ectronics.

Interface....... The computer's *go-between* or translator: any equipment or program which allows different parts to communicate. DOS is a text-based interface between the user and itself, whereas *Windows, System/7*, and *OS/*2 are GUIs (Graphical User Interfaces).

Interlaced..... A term describing how a monitor refreshes the screen. An *interlaced* monitor updates half the screen on each pass (every other row) of **pixels**, each time it *refreshes* the screen. The *refresh* happens 60 to 72 times per second. ➲ Non-Interlaced, **Designing a System**.

Interleave..... On a computer's magnetic Disk it refers to the way the sectors are organized. In 1:1

interleaving the sectors are placed sequentially around the disk, and in 2:1 sectors are staggered to enable the read/write head to access the data in one revolution of the disk. The user can change this ratio with a disk utility program.

Internet......... See "What's Internet?"

ISA............... Pronounced *I-Sa* and *I-S-A*. Acronym for **I**ndustry **S**tandard **A**rchitecture, an open-architecture **bus** design introduced with original IBM *PC*. It can accommodate 8-bit and 16-bit expansion boards. It was superseded in 1988 by **EISA** to compete with IBM's new **MCA** bus. The *Mac* bus is called *NuBus*.

ISDN............. Best known as *"It Still Does Nothing"*, it really means ... **I**ntegrated **S**ervices **D**igital **N**etwork, an AT&T sponsored standard to overcome the limitations of the existing phone line capabilities. It is a totally new concept of what the world's phone system should be: It allows similtaneous voice and data/video transmission over a non-fiber optic (copper) phone line. **Modems** transmit analog signals (sound) over phone lines, whereas ISDN converts it to a digital signal, using a dual pathways for voice and data/video. By early '95 50% of US homes (in large cities) will be ISDN phone capable.

IT .... **I**nformation **T**echnology.

KB................. Acronym for **ki**lo**b**yte.

Kilobyte........ One thousand *bytes* of data (actually 2^{10}=1,024 bytes). See *byte* for details; compare *mega/giga*). [From Greek *khilioi*, thousand]

Kips .... **K**ilos (thousands) of **i**nstructions **p**er second. (See mips).

Landscape	Portrait

Landscape .... 🗎 When printing this refers to the orientation of the text (image) on the page. *Landscape* is oriented horizontally ⇔ and *portrait* is the normal vertical mode ⇕. Landscape printing allows a wide document, such as a spreadsheet, to fit all the columns on one page.

Laptop .... 💻 A personal computer which is small and light enough to be operated from the user's lap comfortably for extended periods. Despite their proportionately high price, they have greatly increased in popularity as they have been reduced in size, while offering the features of a much larger desktop computer. See **Laptops and Notebooks** in the **Senior** section.

LASER........Acronym for **L**ight **A**mplification by **S**timulated **E**mission of **R**adiation. It allows very wide bandwidth communication and low probability of interference, which makes it ideal for fiber optic digital transmissions. The possibility of replacing electronic chips with laser circuits is very bright on the horizon.

Laser printer.............A printer which uses a laser beam and fused toner particles to create an image on paper (or transparency), "electrophotographically". The process is similar to xerographic copier technology. Laser printers were the first to offer near printer quality for the PC market. Commercial print quality is 1280-2450 dpi (dots per inch) compared to 300-1200 dpi for the laser printer; however, this represents a vast improvement in print quality over dot-matrix impact printers, along with increased speed and much lower noise level. Also see the **Senior** chapter.

LCD .... Acronym for **L**iquid **C**rystal **D**isplay. A follow on technology to LED (Light Emitting Diode) which requires much less electricity to power the display. Most commonly used in pocket calculators.

Lithium-ion.. The newest rechargable battery technology for laptops, offering increased operating time. See NiMH.

Log on .... An expression used by computer users who must access a computer by password. It is also used while running a computer/terminal to confirm making a **modem** connection with another computer. When a computer session is finished, the user of a controlled access system must also *Log off*. The expression probably comes from the fact that such controlled access systems keep a computer *log* of all users' activity, usually for security or billing purposes.

Mac .... Abbreviation for *Apple Macintosh* line of personal computers. The *Mac*, introduced in 1984, is a follow-on to the *Apple* series and is based on the *Motorola 68000* series microprocessor. It offers substantial improvements in processing power and the capability of displaying high-

SAME MEANING ... DIFFERENT WORDS

Macintosh	IBM
AppleTalk	LAN
Folder	Directory
Initialize	Format
NuBus	MCA/EISA/*LocalBus*
Trash	Delete

resolution color. Despite a very innovative computer with a wide variety of software, *Mac* computers could not penetrate the main business market until the advent of **Desktop Publishing** in 1985. Utilizing its inherent graphical display abilities (from the game world) and paired with a radically new program called *PageMaker*, which was developed by Seattle-based *Aldus*, the *Mac* finally found a niche in which the IBM *PC* at the time wasn't competitive. *Macs* are strong in graphical business applications such as publishing, designing, architectural, and other creative uses. See *Apple* and *PowerMac*.

MB .... Acronym for **MegaByte** - One million **bytes**. Actually 1,048,576 (2^{20}) **bytes** of

data or approximately 1 million characters. Compare *kilo* & *giga*.
[From Greek *megas*, meaning great].

MCA .... See **M**icro **C**hannel **A**rchitecture.

Megabyte...... One million - actually 1,048,576 **byte**s of data. Abbreviated as **MB**.

Menu............. Each application program has lists of internal commands such as print, save and copy, which can be accessed by a *menu listing*. Such menus come in the form of choices across the top of the screen or in form of *drop-down* boxes.

MHz .... Acronym for **M**ega**H**ertz. One Hertz equals one cycle per second, and one *megahertz* equals one *million* cycles. A tiny current is used in a quartz watch to cause the crystal to vibrate at a known rate, allowing us to measure time by its vibrations per second. Hz is used for screen refresh rates, and MHz is used to measure the *clock speed* of the **CPU** and **Bus**. See *Clock Speed* for details. *Frequency* x wavelength = the velocity of light: 186,000 miles/second. [After H.R.Hertz, 1857-94, a German physicist].

Micro .... Computer: Smallest of the major types of computers, usually a single user system. (See Mainframe, Mini & *PC*)

Micro Channel Architecture .... An IBM **bus** design introduced with its PS/2 line of *PCs* in 1987. It is an improved 16/32-bit bus design which is not compatible with the earlier **ISA** bus. A consortium of nine competitors developed **EISA** in response.

Microprocessor........ *A computer on a* **chip**. Smallest complete microcomputer processor together with all essential circuitry on one *chip*, a thin slice of semiconducting material. A microprocessor is an integrated circuit (IC) that is also referred to as the CPU.

Microsoft....... Now the largest software company in the world. Founded in 1975 by Bill Gates and Paul Allen when they wrote a version of **BASIC**. The basis of the company's success has risen with the incredible popularity of the *IBM compatible PC*, each of which uses the MS-DOS operating system. IBM selected *Microsoft's Disk Operating System* for their *PC* in 1981, which is now up to version 6.0. Building on this foundation, Microsoft developed application programs for the *Apple/Mac* and *IBM PCs*. Prior to the spectacular rise of Microsoft, *Lotus* was the #1 software company, based on revenues. Their most successful application programs include: *Windows*, *Word* (word processing), and *Excel* (spreadsheet). The name *Microsoft* is a contraction of *micro*computer-*soft*ware.

Milli .... One thousandth of a Metric measuring unit (e.g.: millibar, millimeter, millisecond). See nanosecond. [From Latin: *Mille* thousand]

Mini .... Computer. Mid-level of the major types of computers, usually a multi-user system with numerous *dumb* terminals. (See Mainframe & Micro)

Mips .... Millions of instructions per second. Used to rate a Central Processor Unit's (**CPU**) speed - how many instructions (machine code) it can handle in a second. (See Kips)

Modem.......... An electronic device which converts computer digits into sound waves suitable for transmission over phone lines, or digitally via radio and Infrared. Such transmissions may also be encrypted. Also see Baud, bps, & CCITT. Abbreviation of **MO**dulator-**DEM**odulator. Modems are generally referred to by their transfer speeds: 2400, 9600, 14400, 19200 and 28800bps.

Motherboard............ The primary circuit board inside the computer housing upon which all the main electronic circuits are located, including the Central Processing Unit (CPU) *chip*, Random Access Memory (RAM) *chips*, coprocessor (if installed), and the expansion slots.

Mouse .... A hand-held screen pointing device which allows the user to *point and click* rather than typing commands. A (screen-based) extension to the keyboard which operates primarily in a *graphical e*nvironment, such as *Windows*. Though it was developed in the '60s by Xerox, it did not receive widespread acceptance until it was adapted for use on the *Apple* computer by Steven Jobs. See **What's a Mouse**, in the **Freshman** section.

MTBF .... Mean Time Between Failure. Manufactures measure the average working life of products in hours. One hard drive may have a

MTBF of 250,000 hrs, while a less expensive one 175,500 hrs.

Multimedia .... This is the name given to an **application** program which manipulates a vast array of information including still and motion pictures, sound, as well as the regular text. This is covered in greater detail in the tutorial chapters.

Nanosecond .... ⏳ One billionth or 10^{-9} of a second. Electricity, for example, would travel approximately one foot or 1/3 meter, in the course of a nanosecond. Data transfer speed within a computer's hardware (e.g.: **RAM** *chips*) are normally rated in nanoseconds, typically 50 to 120 ns, though 35ns SRAMs are available. Abbreviated as ns. Also see **Index**.

Nerd .... A person who is obsessed with his computer, often with above average IQ, and sometimes exhibiting anti-social behavior. Typical profile: *male, age 9 to 49, impaired eyesight, doesn't dress well, has no time to eat, and doesn't understand why girls are not impressed by his conversation, battery-powered car, or custom 686PC/299MHz/PCI bus with 100 megs of RAM.*

Network........ See "**What is a Network?**"

NiCad .... **Nickel**Cad**mium** battery: the first rechargable battery for laptops.

NiMH..................... **Nickel**Metal**Hydrite** battery: a newer rechargable for laptops. See Lithium-ion.

Non-Interlaced...... A term referring to monitors. An *non-interlaced* monitor updates *every* row of screen **pixels**, each time it *refreshes* the screen, resulting in less screen flicker. The *refresh* happens 60 to 72 times per second (Hz). ⊃ Interlaced, **Designing a System**.

On-the-fly...... An expression to describe a related activity taking place [in the background], in response to the user initiating some action. A good **disk compression** program operates *on-the-fly*: the action of retrieving a compressed file initiates the related (background) activity, of decompressing it.

Online .... An expression to describe the computer being connected, usually via a (modem &) phone *line*, to another compter, or a service such as *AmericaOnline* (adaptation of *"I'm on the line"*).

OS/2 .... ⊞ **O**perating **S**ystem/2. Originally developed to replace MS-DOS as a true *multitasking* graphical operating system. *IBM* backed OS/2 while *Microsoft* continued development of its [interim] *Windows* 286/386 **GUI** interface. The popularity of *Windows* 3.0 and its lower memory requirements, has put the future of OS/2 in doubt.

OverDrive...... An intₑl trademarked name for their *clock-doubler* CPU chip. It allows an i486 PC to be easily upgraded, simply by inserting the *OverDrive* chip into the (required) socket on the **Motherboard**. An *OverDrive* has double or triple the **clock speed** of the existing CPU, however it does not affect the existing CPU ... it is disabled, and the *OverDrive* processor becomes the new

CPU. The clock speed of the motherboard and **bus** remains unchanged, so overall performance is typically less than a double or triple improvement. See **Bus**.

Parallel .... All I/O devices such as the printer, mouse, and modem must communicate with the computer via a *serial* or *parallel* **interface** *port*. A parallel printer cable is also known as a *Centronics* cable.

Parity .... Expressed as Even or Odd Parity, it is an error checking system.   An eighth digit is appended to the usual 7-digit "**byte**", the sum of which must be either even or odd according to its parity. Faulty data is retransmitted.

PC .... Acronym for **P**ersonal **C**omputer. A term introduced by IBM in 1981 to describe a revolutionary development in microcomputers. It was not, however, the first personal computer employing the newly developed **microprocessor**. Both *Apple* and *Osborne* produced 64K models in the late 70s. (See Mainframe, Mini & Micro)

PCMCIA ...... Acronym for **P**ersonal **C**omputer **M**emory **C**ard **I**nternational **A**ssocation.   A new technology of credit-card size, plug-in *cards* weighing just 1 oz., for *laptop* and *notebook* computers.   **Flash Memory**, modems, network connection and even cellular phone links, are some of the cards available.

PDA .... **P**ersonal **D**igital **A**ssistant.   Portable electronic devices that are larger than ectronic

Organizers, possessing more PC-like capabilities, and offering mobile fax & E-Mail communications. Examples include Apple's *Newton*, Motorola's *Envoy* and *Marco*, and Sony's *Magic Link*.

Pentium .... The successor to intel's 80486 microprocessor which was released in '93. Within intel, during its development it was known as the *P5*, however outside Intel it was widely identified as the *80586*. The 3.3 volt, 64-bit *Pentium*™ features 3 million transistors and will run at 2½ times the speed of the 50-MHz *i486*; that's about 100 Million Instructions Per Second. It will also outperform its predecessor, the *i486*, on floating-point calculations by more than 4 to 1. intel has discontinued the use of numbers in naming its microprocessors to avoid confusion with competing brands such as *Cyrix*, who use the same model numbers. *i486*™ is an intel TradeMark, but *486* cannot be trade marked. The original version ran at 60MHz which has been *tweeked* to 66, 75, 90 (P90), 100, 120, and 150MHz.

PIM .... Personal Information Manager. Software programs such as Lotus *Organizer* which aid people who track sales, contact activity, customers, appointments, travel, etc.

Pixel .... A word derived from the contraction of two words: **Pic**ture **El**ement. Monitors display graphic images by thousands of tiny dots or *pixels*. The closer these pixels, the better the picture quality. On color monitors each pixel is actually composed of three color pixels: red, green, and blue.

Plug 'n Play.. A standard created by Microsoft and Intel to make the addition of plug-in boards less hassle. *Hot swapping* of components will be possible without rebooting. Abbreviated as PnP.

Point size ...... A typographical (printing) measurement where one point equals 1/72 of an inch. The size of the characters you are reading is 13 points (normally abbreviated as pts.). Here are some examples of other point sizes: 6 Points, 12 Points, 20 Points. See Font, Typeface. Diplomatic messages are routinely sent on microdots, about the size of a punctuation mark, and placed somewhere in a letter.

Pop-Up .... ✍ Nick-name for **TSR**s (See TSR).

Port .... All external devices are connected to the computer via a *port* or plug-in point, normally at the back of the computer box. Ports may be either *serial* or *parallel*.

| Landscape | Portrait |

Portrait .... 🖹 When printing, this refers to the orientation of the text or image on the page. *Portrait* is the normal printing orientation ↕ for letters and most documents: *landscape* orientes the image horizontally ⇔.

PostScript ..... A scalable outline font language (software) pioneered by *Adobe Systems*. *PS* treats text and graphics alike, allowing infinite variation in sizes of each font with very high quality. It is *the standard* in the printing industry and it was used to produce this book. It also features ***WYSIWYG*** (what-you-see-is-what-you-get) on the screen in the *Windows* environment. Also see *TrueType*.

PowerPC ...... First there was *Apple*, then came the *PC* from *IBM*, and a multitude of clone companies. *Apple* grew into the *Mac* and is still having trouble holding its market share against the popularity of the *Intel/DOS/Windows* based PC (IBM & clones). The *Mac's* operating system (System7) and hardware design is not "open" like the *IBM PC* & company, but they are about to license clones. To compete with the *Microsoft/Intel* (software/hardware) dominance, three big players, *Apple, IBM and Motorola*, formed a consortium to produce an advanced PC with features beyond even the future *686* CPU, voilà ... the *PowerPC*. Its Motorola microprocessor needs software applications written specifically for it to take full advantage of its "power", however its backers believe one of its great advantages is that it can use most of the popular operating systems, such as *Mac, OS/2* for *PowerPC*, and *Windows NT*, and therefore many of today's applications. The *PowerMac* from *Apple* is the first in this series to ship.

Processor ...... The Central **Process**ing Unit (CPU), or computer "brain". The modern PC is based on a (tiny) *micro*processor.

Prodigy .... An on-line information service accessed via a **modem**. Offers satellite weather, stock quotes, shopping, airline ticket reservations, bulletin board (**EBB**), and a host of other services. See EBB & Internet.

RAM .... **R**andom **A**ccess **M**emory. The computer's *working memory* connected to the Central Processing Unit (**CPU**), normally requiring electricity to function. Digital information can be *written* to, and retrieved from, RAM *chips*. The computer's **operating system**, the core of the **application** program, and the data you are working on are all held in RAM. In short, the human equivalent is the memory part of the brain. RAM *chips* are rated in **nanosecond**s (ns), a lower number indicating a faster rate of data transfer (typically 80 to 150ns). The amount of RAM is measured in megabytes (MB), typically from 2 to 16MB.

Record .... Records are the building blocks of a database **file**. A person's last name, first name, phone number, salary, start date, and address are all associated pieces of information that make up one record. The parts of the record (name, phone, etc.), are called *fields*.

RISC .... Acronym for **R**educed **I**nstruction **S**et **C**omputer. A rival design for microprocessors to int**e**l's CISC (Complex Instruction-Set Computing). RISC is used in only 11% of desktop computer *chips*, compared with 89% for CISC.

ROM .... Acronym for **R**ead **O**nly **M**emory. Memory *chips* which the computer can *read from*, but not *write to* (store data). They differ from regular **RAM** chips, which are *read/write*. Plug-in *ROM chips* containing **application** software such as Lotus 1-2-3 are used in some *laptops* to save **Hard Disk** space.

FILE DIRECTORY or FOLDER
(*Inverted tree*)

Root Directory .... A **disk** may contain many different *directories* or logical divisions (as opposed to physical), and the *directory* from which all others stem, is called the *root directory*. A **hard disk** directory is often represented like an upside down tree going from the trunk (root directory) to branches (sub-directory) to leaves (files). The *Mac* term for *Directory* is *Folder*, as a directory is the computer's version of a File Folder.

Save............... 🖫 Normally expressed as *to save [one's work]* ... *saving* copies the active user file (what you see on screen) from **RAM** onto a permanent storage media, usually the **Hard Disk**. Each time a file [with the same name] is *saved* it automatically *overwrites* the existing file.

SCSI.............. Pronounced *Scuzzy*: Acronym for **S**mall **C**omputer **S**ystem **I**nterface. It offers advantages such as speed and fewer compatibility problems, compared to **IDE**. An industry standard which specifies mechanical, electrical, and other standards for the connection of hard drives and other drives (CD-ROM, etc.) to PCs. It allows transfer rates of 5MBps or 10 Mbps (megabytes/second) . This parrallel connection was developed for the *Mac*, but is also used by *IBM* compatibles and UNIX computers. *SCSI-1 & SCSI-2* both have a max transfer rate of 5mbps. *Fast SCSI-2* has a rate of 10MBps. *Fast & Wide SCSI-2* doubles the bandwidth from 8 bits to 16 bits, resulting in a further doubling of the max transfer rate to 20mbps. SCSI transfer speeds often exceed the disk drive's "read/write" speed, in which case the speed of the disk's function determines the transfer rate. Disk Arrays overcome this problem by allowing the interface to write to multiple disks, which it sees "as one disk".

Sector............. A 512-byte unit that represents the smallest amount of data that can be written to, or read from, a **disk**. Sectors make up the concentric circles or tracks around a disk. See the chapter on Magnetic Disks for more details.

Semiconductor......... Metals are typically good conductors, and wood typically a good insulator. However, there are substances such as silicon, which are neither good conductors or insulators, and these are known as semiconductors. Such material is used to make **transistors**, the basic building block of modern computers.

Serial............. All **I/O** (input/output) devices such as the printer, mouse, and modem, must communicate with the computer via a *serial* or **parallel** (**interface**) **port**.

SIMMS .... Acronym for **S**ingle **I**n-line **M**emory **M**odule **S**ystem. SIMMS are simply 3 or 9 **DRAM**s on a single *chip* which allows more **RAM** memory directly on the *motherboard*. The *motherboard* is designed to accept either DRAMs or SIMMS/DRAMs. SIMMS come in 1, 4, 8, 16 & 32MB configurations.

Slot .... Expansion *slots* are where expansion *boards* are plugged in, usually located on the *motherboard*. *Slots* allow peripheral devices and memory to be added to a computer, providing increased flexibility in the hardware configuration. See **The parts of a Computer** in the **FRESHMAN** chapter.

Sound card... An optional card which plugs into the computer's **motherboard**. Allows full audio features of **multimedia** CDs, embedded speech in documents, and **speech recognition** systems.

Spooler .... A software **buffer** or **interface** which feeds a device such as a printer. A print *spooler* typically holds the print data in **RAM** after you activate the print command or as a *temp* file on the **Hard Disk**, *spooling* it to the printer at a rate the printer can accept the data. *Windows* calls this queuing, and it is handled automatically by *Print Manager*, which operates in the background.

Spreadsheet.............. See "**What's a Spreadsheet?**"

SRAM........... Pronounced *S-RAM*: **S**tatic **RAM** (Random Access Memory) *chips*. Considerably faster and more expensive than **DRAM**s with the advantage that memory does not have to be refreshed. They are made from Gallium Arsenide rather than silicon. A 1**MB** SRAM with 1**ns** access time has been developed for the military. (See RAM)

Surge Protector .... An optional external device which protects electrical equipment (computer, printer, etc.) from *surges and spikes* commonly found in AC circuits. Inexpensive & highly recomended. Most are sacrificial, but don't indicate when their sacrificial circuits are no longer protecting. A **UPS** offers more complete protection.

System 7.5 ..... The latest Operating System for the *Apple **Mac**intosh* line of personal computers. It features *Virtual Memory* and *Multitasking*. By combining *DOS 6.2* and *Windows 3.1*, the IBM world now has an equivalent to *System 7*.

Telephony..... A term coined by Sun Microsystems, it means the integration of the telephone *into* the computer.

TPI................ Acronym for **T**racks **p**er **I**nch. A measure of the closeness of the *tracks (*concentric circles - like a *bull's eye*) which divides up the surface of a magnetic **disk**. The higher the TPI, the more data that can be stored on a disk. A *diskette* could have 135 TPI while a *Hard Disk* may have 600 or more.

Transistor..... Abbreviation for TRANSfer resISTOR, an important electronic **semiconductor** device invented by three scientists at *Bell Labs* in 1948. The trio was awarded the *Nobel* prize for physics in 1956 in recognition of this revolutionary development. Early *transistors* used a pin-head sized piece of germanium encased in a tiny metal cylinder only a ½" long. Vacuum tubes cost 75¢ then compared with early *transistors* which cost $8, in part because of the germanium, which cost more than gold per ounce. In 1954 *Texas Instruments*, better known as *TI*, produced an inexpensive *transistor* by using silicon and improving the manufacturing process. Silicon is the main element of ordinary sand and the second most abundant chemical after oxygen. By replacing vacuum tubes with these solid-state devices, power consumption, heat output, and size were slashed. The first widespread use of transistors was in portable radios which became known as a *transistor radio*. **Microprocessor**s, or *computers on a chip*, are made up of thousands of *transistors* and other miniaturized electronic devices on a tiny silicon *chip* the size of a baby's fingernail. A transistor is made like a sandwich, consisting of one layer of **semiconductor** material between two layers of a different type of semiconducting material. By blocking electric current or allowing it to pass, you create an *on-off* switch, which is used in a computer's *true/false* operations. *Transistors* can also boost a small voltage. See also **IC**.

True Type .... A scalable font system packaged with *Windows 3.1*. It offers **WYSIWYG** (what-you-see-is-what-you-get) on the screen, and professional looking printed text. See also *PostScript*.

TSR............... ✍   An acronym for **T**erminate and **S**tay **R**esident. Used in the MS-DOS enviroment they are popularly known as *Pop-Up* or *Memory Resident* programs because they reside in **RAM** (Random Access Memory). This enables them to be activated instantly rather than having to wait while they load. Normally only one application program (e.g.: word processor) resides in memory at a time; however small utility programs such as appointment reminders, calendars, calculators, and screen savers can also be loaded and left in a *sleep mode* until activated, usually by a ***hot key***. Software conflicts can occur, as TSRs reside in RAM and they can degrade the performance of the primary **application**.

Typeface....... It's the face design of characters. It is the most distinguishing feature of a particular font. The text you are reading is a classic *typeface* called Times Roman, which was designed for the *London Times* in 1932. The *style* of a typeface can be normal, *italic*, or **bold**. The following are examples of some popular *typefaces*, some of which are used in this book; they are all 13 points in size: Courier,   **Dom Casual 99**, Helvetica 123, **JUNIPER 789,** *Present 456,* Script 911, Rotunda. ➲ also Font & Point size.

UPC .... **U**niform **P**rice **C**ode enables computerized pricing and inventory control. Usually displayed in **Bar Code** format on supermarket items, paperback books, and magazines. Each UPC represents a unique number [issued by the Uniform Code Council].

UPS .... Acronym for **U**ninterruptible **P**ower **S**upply. An external device between the main power supply and the computer which *kicks-in* automatically, when even a microsecond interruption occurs in the electrical power coming into the computer. Some UPSs also "filter" the incoming power, suppress **surge**s, and boost low voltage, thereby protecting the computer's sensitive circuitry. Critical data can be lost during a momentary power outage if the disk drive is saving or **modem** transfers are in progress. APC (800/800-4272) is highly recommended as they offer an excellent range of budget and ti-tech UPSs.

Vaporware ... New software programs or major revisions, announced by the company but which fail to appear on schedule.

Virtual Memory .... A technique for expanding the computer's RAM *artificially*. A portion of the Hard Disk is set aside, and when large files are open, the bulk of that file is stored in Virtual Memory (on disk), rather than in RAM. This allows the computer to *function* as if it had 5 or 10 megabytes of RAM memory, when in fact it may have just 2. It is less expensive than buying more RAM, but considerably slower. It's an an abbreviation of an early expression ... *it's virtually [RAM] memory.*

VGA.............. Acronym for **V**ideo **G**raphics **A**rray. **IBM**'s third generation graphics standard for the *PC* monitor introduced in 1987. Offers 16 colors and 640x480 pixel resolution. *Expanded VGA* is an improved standard and *Super VGA* offers 256 colors at 1024 x 768 resolution. See XGA.

Wait states.... Cycles where the processor (CPU) does nothing. When memory cannot keep up with the processor, the processor must insert *wait states*. The nanosecond rating of memory chips must be correctly matched to the CPU and clock speed to avoid unnecessary *wait states*.

Word processor... A new **software** technology to create and revise documents with computers. For a detailed discussion see page 61.

Workstation ..... A *supermicro* computer based on an int₍e₎l *386* or faster microprocessor, with enhanced processing features often used in an engineering role or **CAD**. Prior to its development, a **minicomputer**, or even a **mainframe**, was required.

WYSIWYG .... Pronounced *wizzy-wig*, it is an acronym for *What-You-See-Is-What-You-Get*. Its an expression to describe the closeness between what you see on the screen and what the printed document looks like. All *Mac* and *Windows* **applications** offer *WYSIWYG*. It is very useful in **word processing, desktop publishing** and any design work to see an accurate presentation of fonts, point size, and how margins will affect the layout.

WWW........................ Acronym for **W**orld**W**ide **W**eb, which refers to all the linked **databases** available via **Internet**. *Netscape, MacWeb, Mosaic, and WinWeb* are graphical interfaces (front doors) for Internet.

XGA............... Acronym for **E**xtended **G**raphics **A**rray. Latest video standard from *IBM* announced in 1990 for their high-end *XP* series of *PCs*. *XGA* displays double the number of screen pixels compared to standard *VGA*.

Think I'll learn how to fly next ...

Computer Equivalents		
Computer Term	*Automobile*	*Human*
Hardware	Automobile	Body
Software	Fuel	Language
Intel	Gasoline Engine[2]	English
Motorola	Diesel Engine[3]	French
Input	Accelerator pedal	Listening
Output	Speedometer	Talking
CPU	Engine	Brain
Bus	Electrical wiring	Nerves
Clock speed	RPM	Heart beat
Bit rating	Carburetor/Injector	Food portion
RAM	Engine size	Body size
Hard Disk	Size of fuel tank	Memory

---

[2] The most popular type of internal combustion engine.

[3] The analogy here is that it is like the gasoline engine as it has all the same moving parts, but is designed to run on a different fuel, which is compared to the Operating System.

The Index provides a complete cross-reference catalog to selected terms from the four tutorial chapters, and all the entries found in the Terminology Section.

CONFIDENTIAL
NOTES

SELF TEST

1.   I have read the entire book and understand:
    a. ❑   most of it (Completely *Normal*)
    b. ❑   all of it (Magna Cum Laude)
    c. ❑   none of it (Attemptus Meritorious).

2.   I plan to:
    a. ❑   start using the computer I bought
    b. ❑   take the kids computer
    c. ❑   buy a computer

3. ❑   I can now turn on the computer without asking my teenager for help.

4. ❑   I can delete a file without seeing smoke coming out of my own ears.

5. ❑   I wrote a letter to the President using the word processor:
    a. ❑   I also printed it.

6. ❑   *Windows*:
    a. ❑   Thrills me like a roller coaster ride
    b. ❑   Reminds me of rush hour traffic.

7. ❑   I plan to access the *Internet* this year.

Date _____   Signed _____